TABLE O

D1553881

PART THREE:
THE PENTECOSTAL/CHARISMATIC MOVEMENT
IN THE LIGHT OF SCRIPTURE

INTRODUCTION

On New Year's Eve, December 31, 1900, just a few hours before the start of the 20th century, a religious movement began that would have a tremendous impact on the religious world. Begun in very inauspicious circumstances, this movement has influenced more lives and done more to shape religious thinking than any other since the Protestant Reformation.

For one hundred years, the movement has been spreading throughout the world. For the first 50 or 60 years, it was called the Pentecostal movement. People who received the Pentecostal "spirit" joined together in churches and denominations devoted to Pentecostal teaching. Pentecostal churches were broadly shunned by the middle and upper classes of society as being anti-intellectual and even weirdly elitist.

In the 1960s, however, something happened that the members of the original Pentecostal churches probably never thought they would see. The movement spilled over into traditional Christian denominations. Large numbers of people experienced the Pentecostal "baptism in the Holy Spirit" and speaking in tongues. The Pentecostal movement had produced a clone, the charismatic movement, which swept like a fast-rising tide into every major denomination in America, Catholic and Protestant. It lent an aura of sophistication and respectability to some of the very teachings and practices that had kept many people at a distance. The rapid growth of Pentecostal churches and the even more rapid growth of the charismatic spirit within traditional denominations have given rise to a movement that Christians must come to grips with.

Unprecedented growth

A brief look at the statistics will show us how quickly the Pentecostal/charismatic movement has spread and why it is important for us to know something about it. Richard

Ostling, writing in *Time,* concluded that the growth of Pentecostal groups far outstrips that of all other Christian groups. In 1980 there were an estimated 345 million Protestants worldwide, with Pentecostals (not including charismatics) comprising the largest denominational subgroup, numbering over 51 million members.[1]

Of the Pentecostal denominations, the Assemblies of God (AOG) is the largest. In 1914 it numbered ten thousand members in the United States. By 1940 it had grown to two hundred thousand, and by the early 1980s it had grown to ten million members worldwide.[2] It is predicted that by 2000 or shortly thereafter, the AOG will be larger than the Episcopal church or the Presbyterian church (USA).

Starting in the early 1960s, the charismatic renewal movement shared the same spectacular growth. In 1967 Pentecostalism poured into the Roman Catholic Church—a truly amazing development. By mid 1988, 12% of all Roman Catholics in the world could be given the Pentecostal/charismatic label.[3]

Dr. David B. Barrett's *Global Expansion of the Renewal across the 20th Century, A.D. 1400–2000,* helps us put the movement into perspective. According to Barrett, who in 1982 published a nation-by-nation survey of church demographics, in 1993 there were 429,523,000 Pentecostals/charismatics.[4] He estimates that 70 percent of all church growth worldwide is among Pentecostal/charismatic groups. He notes that 54 thousand people a day, or over 19 million people a year, become Pentecostal/charismatic. Two-thirds of the current global evangelization plans can be credited to Pentecostal/charismatic churches or church agencies. They account for one hundred new mission agencies in the Western world and over three hundred in the Third World.[5] Among the fastest growing churches in 1990 was World Changers Ministries, a black charismatic congregation in Atlanta, Georgia. The Church of God in Christ, a black Pentecostal group based in Memphis, Tennessee, is reported to be the fastest growing denomination in the United States.[6]

Barrett estimates that by 2000 there will be a total of 562,526,000 Pentecostal/charismatic church members worldwide. This, he points out, will represent 28.6 percent of the membership of Christian churches. He further points out that there will be another 56,800,000 Pentecostals/charismatics who are unaffiliated with any church, bringing the total to 619,326,000 professing Pentecostals/charismatics.

How accurate are these figures? That is difficult to determine. However, they do illustrate a point that is indisputable. The Pentecostal/charismatic movement is a force to be reckoned with. It invites—even demands—close and thorough examination. Its history, teachings, philosophies, practices, claims, strengths, and weaknesses all must be evaluated in the light of God's Word.

Our course as Christians is clear, for the Lord's apostle has warned, "Test the spirits to see whether they are from God" (1 John 4:1). God's Word is the only basis of our Christian religion. It is our spiritual chart and compass to which we must turn to find direction also in settling the questions and issues raised by the Pentecostal/charismatic movement.

Part One

THE HISTORY OF PENTECOSTALISM:

OLD AND NEW

1

PENTECOSTAL FERVOR BEFORE 1900

Before we speak about the outbreak and growth of the modern Pentecostal/charismatic movement, it would be good to examine church history. The modern Pentecostal/charismatic movement puts much emphasis on "experiencing" the Holy Spirit. Pentecostals and charismatics look for signs that the Holy Spirit is working in the believer, his work being manifested by supernatural charismatic gifts, especially speaking in tongues. Are there parallels in church history?

Did the early church, the Middle Age church, or the church at the time of the Reformation stress a "baptism of the Holy Spirit" accompanied by sensational works such as speaking in tongues (glossolalia), prophesying, and healing? What about the post-Reformation church? Were there groups that taught that the church should reenact Acts 2, with each believer experiencing his own little Pentecost? A study of church history reveals that the modern Pentecostal/charismatic phenomenon is nothing new. When and where this phenomenon is found, however, will help us establish a pattern that will be useful when we analyze the modern movement.

The apostolic church

Some supernatural charismatic gifts continued to be practiced in the church for a period of time after the apostles had died. The gift of speaking in tongues disappeared quite early. This would agree with the lesser value the apostle Paul placed on speaking in tongues and with the fact that speaking in tongues often gave rise to confusion, jealousy, and dissension in the early church. It was also a gift that was easy to counterfeit. Gifts such as healings seemed to remain for a longer time.

From the apostles to the Reformation

Clement I, bishop of Rome (ca. 91–100), was the first of the apostolic church fathers. He supposedly traveled with Paul and Peter. He recorded what he considered to be a "plentiful outpouring of the Holy Spirit upon all."[1] While he did not specifically mention supernatural charismatic gifts of the Spirit, some think he alluded to them. If this is so, Clement may have been referring to some who were still alive in his day to whom the apostles had conferred miracle-working power by the laying on of hands.

Another apostolic church father, Ignatius, who was martyred by Trajan in 107, wrote a letter to the church at Smyrna in which he concluded that the church was blessed with every good gift. Perhaps he also was referring to gifts of supernatural character.[2]

By the second century, the number of people upon whom the apostles had laid hands and bestowed miracle-working power was dwindling. Only the apostle John lived to the end of the first century (or close to it).

Justin Martyr (ca. 100–166), a so-called Christian philosopher, claimed that miraculous powers such as healing and the ability to exorcise demons were practiced by Christians in the face of pagans who were powerless to imitate them. Justin claimed that Christians were also endowed with the gift of prophecy. Yet he referred to "no particular instance of an exercise of miraculous power."[3] In Justin's description of an early church service, he made no mention of anyone speaking in tongues or performing miracles.[4]

The Shepherd of Hermas (ca. 100–140), a deeply religious man, wrote a Christian allegory in which he incorporated visions he supposedly had seen.[5]

Irenaeus (ca. 115–200), bishop of Lyons and a highly respected theologian of the early church, claimed that Christians exercised miraculous powers in his day. He wrote about healings, prophecies, insights into secrets, exorcisms of demons, speaking in tongues, and the dead being raised to life.[6] Yet he was the only one to report these phenomena in the early church, and he himself does not claim to have witnessed anyone being raised from the dead. Irenaeus, like Justin, "speaks altogether generally, adducing no specific cases, but ascribing miracle-working to 'all who were truly disciples of Jesus,' each according to the gift he had received."[7] Yet Irenaeus, in his writings, could have been referring to the practices of the Montanists, a heretical Pentecostal sect of that day.

Benjamin Warfield concludes, "The writings of the so-called Apostolic Fathers contain no clear and certain allusions to miracle-working or to the exercise of the charismatic gifts" in their day.[8]

A converted pagan priest named Montanus began opposing the secularization and worldliness of the church in the latter part of the second century. Montanus claimed to possess the gift of prophecy. He prophesied in the first person, causing many to believe that he was actually the manifestation of the Comforter promised by Christ in John 14 and 16. According to Eusebius, a historian in the early church, Montanus would suddenly fall into an ecstatic frenzy and utter strange things. Eusebius quotes Apolinarius, bishop of Hierapolis, who maintained that Montanus' prophesying was "in a manner contrary to the constant custom of the Church handed down by tradition from the beginning."[9] According to Apolinarius, the Montanists "talked wildly and unreasonably and strangely."[10] The followers of Montanus claimed to have received visions and at times subordinated the apostles' teachings to these revelations. Though Montanism became widespread, it eventually lost its "Pentecostal" character, and prophetic tongues ceased to be mentioned in their writings. Finally, in the sixth century, this ancient sect disappeared.

Tertullian (ca. 150–230), considered one of the greatest teachers of the Latin Church, was enticed by the asceticism of the Montanists. He reported that the Christians of his time were daily expelling demons from the possessed.[11] He also adduced "one case of a prophetically gifted woman."[12]

Another church father, Origen (ca. 185–254), reported that miraculous signs given by the Holy Spirit were less pronounced in his day and that, while there were still visible traces of the Holy Spirit's presence in divine healings, they were becoming less common. Origen flatly denied that living Christians still spoke real prophecies, whether in intelligible or ecstatic speech.

Gregory (ca. 210–270), bishop of Neocaesarea, was known in his day as The Wonder Worker. He was credited with performing many different miracles. Yet the record of his works seems so embellished that it is hard to determine how much is fact and how much is fable.

The same is true of another church father, Hilary (ca. 291–371). Claims about his supernatural works seem to be a mixture of fact and legend.

Ambrose (ca. 340–397), bishop of Milan and staunch defender of orthodox Christianity, is said to have cured the sick and expelled demons. We don't know if there is any truth to these claims. He himself expressed surprise at the report of miraculous events accompanying the discovery of the bodies of two martyrs. When he heard the news, he cried out, "The miracles of old time . . . are come again."[13]

Martin of Tours (ca. 316–400) was one of the founders of the Celtic church. Many have shaken their heads in disbelief while hearing about Martin's deeds as they are reported by Sulpitius Severus in the second book of his *Dialogues*.[14] While many miracles were ascribed to Martin, fact cannot be separated from fiction. We should bear in mind that he lived in an age when "pious" legends were considered a valid remedy against claims made by pagans and heretics.

Warfield gives us the big picture: "There is little or no evidence at all for miracle-working during the first fifty years of the post-Apostolic church; it is slight and unimportant for the next fifty years; it grows more abundant during the [third] century."[15] He states that by the end of the third century, the records show an ever-increasing stream of the miraculous but "without a single writer having claimed himself to have wrought a miracle of any kind or having ascribed miracle-working to any known name in the church, and without a single instance having been recorded in detail."[16]

However, things change in the fourth century. The greatest writers record instances of miracle-working they themselves witnessed "with the greatest circumstantiality."[17] Warfield concludes, "Thus, if the evidence is worth anything at all, instead of a regularly progressing decrease, there was a steadily growing increase of miracle-working from the beginning on."[18]

These testimonies to miraculous occurrences in the fourth century are by no means proven historical fact. Most of them seem to have arisen from fertile imaginations. Warfield writes:

> What are we to think of these miracles? There is but one historical answer which can be given. They represent an infusion of heathen modes of thought into the church. . . . Every religious possession the heathen had, indeed, the Christians, it may be said broadly, transferred to themselves and made their own. As one of the results, the whole body of heathen legends, in one way or another, reproduced themselves on Christian ground.[19]

Warfield summarizes the situation this way: "In one word, what we find, when we cast our eye over the whole body of Christian legends, growing up from the third century down through the Middle Ages, is merely a reproduction, in Christian form, of the motives, and even the very incidents, which already meet us in the legends of heathendom."[20]

While there were some reports of speaking in tongues in the Roman Catholic Church from the postapostolic period to the church at the time of the Reformation, there were no genuine manifestations of tongues-speaking. Tongues-speaking is supposedly a long-standing tradition in the monasteries of the Eastern Orthodox (Greek) church. Still, the history of Eastern Orthodoxy is marred in general by reports of strange and excessive behavior in the monasteries.[21]

During these years there were also reports of healings, visions, and the dead being raised to life. Yet many of these "miracles" were done in connection with relics taken from dead saints (the bones of Saint Stephen were extremely popular in this regard). This was a far cry from the miracles performed in the apostolic age!

During this period many individuals and groups claimed personal, direct, inner revelations from the Holy Spirit, also referred to as an "internal" word. Not infrequently, however, those who claimed to have had such "immediate" revelations from God also disclaimed the Holy Scripture as the Holy Spirit's tool to reveal God's truth. Some considered Holy Scripture to be of only minor importance.[22]

The Reformation era

During the days of the Reformation, a radical reform group emerged. Its members were called Anabaptists and were similar to Pentecostals. They thought Luther and the other reformers were not going far enough in their attempts to reform the church. The reformers called these agitators *schwaermer,* which we might translate "enthusiasts." These enthusiasts rejected infant Baptism and rebaptized members who had been baptized as infants. (*Anabaptist* means "rebaptizer.") They disdained state churches and created their own church—a new family of holy persons. And they subordinated the Holy Scriptures and the sacraments to a higher guidance, an "inner light" from the Holy Spirit.[23] The Anabaptists believed that each member of the family of holy persons was meant to enjoy the gift of prophecy and had the skill to interpret divine revelations.

The radical reformers came in many different stripes and shades—all of them a mar on the Reformation and many of them a blight on society as well. Some were called quietists.

They did not foment revolution or believe in the use of force but were content to spread their doctrines by quiet and peaceful means. Their leader was Menno Simons, who still has followers today, called Mennonites. On the other hand, the "radical," or revolutionary, Anabaptists were fanatical and fostered revolt against the state and against ecclesiastical authority.[24]

The Anabaptist movement began in Zwickau, Saxony. Three members of the group were expelled from Zwickau and went to Wittenberg, the home of the Reformation. These Zwickau prophets, as they were called, began to preach about their heavenly visions and revelations. These and other "heavenly prophets," as Luther dubbed them, aroused and excited the citizens of Wittenberg. Their chief prophet, Thomas Muenzer, boasted of having prophetic visions and dreams and of receiving direct communication from God.[25]

Caspar of Schwenkfeld in Silesia is another man who claimed to receive direct revelations from God. He also is noted for his doctrinal errors. He denied justification by faith, he attacked Luther's position that the Word of God is the only source and norm of faith, he denied that the Holy Spirit works through the sacraments, he refused to baptize children, and in general he took doctrinal positions that were in direct opposition to Bible truth. Some of his followers migrated to America early in the 18th century. They settled in counties around Philadelphia, Pennsylvania, where their descendants can still be found.

One of Luther's own coworkers, Andreas Karlstadt, became an enthusiast and caused the Reformer no little grief. Luther judged the spirit of Karlstadt and of the other "heavenly prophets" as not being the spirit of God but of the devil.[26] The *schwaermer* wanted to take the lead in reforming the church. Their cry was, "The Spirit! The Spirit!" Luther replied, "I will not follow where their spirit leads." On another occasion he said, "I slap your spirit on the snout!"

The years after the Reformation

The Cévennol prophets

In 1685 when the Edict of Nantes, which allowed religious freedom, was revoked by the French king Louis XIV, a new wave of terror broke out against the French Huguenots. These Protestants, who lived in the Cévennes mountains in the southeastern part of France, put up a stiff resistance to the Catholic forces of the king. At the height of the brutality imposed on them, the people—males and females, young and old—underwent a remarkable ecstatic experience. They heard music such as the singing of psalms and strange sounds and saw visions and apparitions. They spoke in tongues and prophesied. They exhorted the people to repent and denounced the Roman Catholic Church, which in itself was not unusual; nevertheless, they spoke in eloquent French, a language completely unknown to them. Their religious frenzy was accompanied by severe physical contortions, foaming at the mouth, and sobbing.[27]

This movement continued for over ten years, and finally it turned political. The Cévennol people attacked the French government but were defeated and punished.

The Jansenists

A few decades later, an emotional outbreak occurred among the Jansenists, a French Catholic holiness sect. Those involved had revolted against the spiritual coldness and immorality of the Jesuits. In 1731 the Jansenists began to experience speaking in tongues. Their tongues-speaking was described as a "meaningless torrent of syllables."[28]

The Ranters

We also discover Pentecostal-type movements in England during the post-Reformation period. The Ranters were religious radicals of the mid 1600s. They spoke in tongues. Like the Anabaptists, they gained an unsavory reputation for themselves and were frequently accused of lewdness and irreligious actions and utterances. According to a contemporary, Samuel Fisher, some of them even went so far as to claim to be Christ and God.

The Quakers

The Quakers arose in England about the middle of the 17th century. The Religious Society of Friends, as the members called themselves, was founded by George Fox, who believed that he received revelations from God. Divorcing "Christian truth" from Holy Scripture, he laid all the emphasis on an "inner light," which he claimed came by direct inspiration of the Holy Spirit. Following his leadership, the Quakers regarded the inner light to be superior to Holy Scripture, as is evident in their assemblies. The members gather and sit quietly until one of them feels moved by the Holy Spirit to speak.[29]

The Shakers

In 1747 the Shaker movement began in England. In 1774 the Shakers migrated to America and settled in Watervliet, New York. The Shakers spoke in tongues, sometimes accompanied by singing and dancing. In their ecstasy, they composed many hymns, but without recognizable linguistic form or meaning.[30] People were convinced of the validity of Shaker doctrine and practice from the so-called gifts of the Spirit they displayed. These included, according to one observer, a variety of marvelous operations, signs and visions, as well as speaking in tongues and prophesying.

Pietism in Scandinavia

In Scandinavia religious revival accompanied the pietistic movement. Pietism's emphasis on religious experience sometimes gave it a Pentecostal flavor. In northern Sweden the pietists were called readers. Some of them sought Pentecostal experiences, including speaking in tongues. In another area of Sweden, Smaland, a large number of people of all ages went into trances, saw visions, jerked, contorted, shouted, and groaned.[31]

A leader of the pietistic movement in Finland, Paavo Ruotsalainen, emphasized looking to Christ in faith, trusting Christ to act in one's life, and experiencing an "inner feeling" of grace.[32]

Pentecostal-type outbreaks in Russia and Armenia

In 1855 Russia experienced a great revival that included speaking in tongues. This movement spilled over into Armenia. Though of great intensity and scope, it was short lived.

There was another movement 25 years later. It was similar to the first and also included speaking in tongues. A small group of Armenian Presbyterians joined together to form a Pentecostal worship group. Included in this Pentecostal group was the Shakarian family. Beginning in 1900 many of these Russians and Armenians immigrated to America. After settling in Los Angeles, the Shakarian family opened their home to Armenian and Russian Pentecostals for group worship. The Shakarian name will come up again.[33] The family had connections with the Azusa Street mission in Los Angeles, and Demos Shakarian became the founder of the Full Gospel Business Men's Fellowship International.

Others

There are other examples in church history of individuals or groups that have spoken in tongues. For example, in 1854 V. P. Simmons reported tongues-speaking in New England. Elder F. G. Mathewson spoke in tongues, and Elder Edward Burnham interpreted.[34] In 1875 R. B. Swan, a pastor in Providence, Rhode Island, together with his wife and some others, spoke a few words in what they referred to as an "unknown tongue."[35] A few years later, in 1879, W. Jethro Walthall in Arkansas spoke in tongues yet knew nothing of the Holy Spirit's giving of this gift in Bible times.[36]

The Mormons

Although not a part of the Christian church, the Mormon church used speaking in tongues. In article 7 of the official digest of Mormon doctrine, Joseph Smith promoted the gift of tongues and the interpretation of tongues. Tongues-speaking was finally discouraged in public because of the ridicule it brought from those outside of the Mormon church. Heber Grant, the seventh president of the church, and his wife experienced speaking in tongues and interpreting tongues. He subsequently called the lack of the gift of tongues and interpretation a sign of the lack of true faith.

Summary

From what we have seen, we can make the following generalizations. Tongues-speaking seems to have disappeared very early from the church, except for spurious manifestations of ecstatic tongues in the ancient Pentecostal sect of the Montanists. In later church history, tongues-speaking is confined almost entirely to heretical sects and non-Christian groups. At times it was evident in groups undergoing severe religious persecution. In historical accounts speaking in tongues is generally confined to a form of irrational speech, often in the company of bizarre conduct.

References to exorcisms, healings, and other miracles, including restoring the dead to life, multiplied in the centuries following the apostolic period. However, the reports of these are subject to great exaggeration and to conflicting testimonies, and they often appear to mimic the stories and legends of heathendom.

The true miraculous gifts of the Spirit were confined mostly to the apostolic age and carried over to some extent in the postapostolic age. Genuine displays of supernatural charismata—displays that can be properly identified and validated—are missing from most of church history. Those modern-day Pentecostals and charismatics who claim that they are sharing in a long tradition reaching back to the early church cannot prove that claim from church history.

2

THE ARRIVAL OF MODERN PENTECOSTALISM

In the last chapter, we examined what role charismatic gifts played in the church of the past. In this chapter we will again survey church history, but with a more narrow focus. The modern Pentecostal/charismatic movement grew out of forces already at work in the United States. In the last half of the 1800s, the pressure that was building in the holiness movement was finally released in the Pentecostal movement. Taking it back one step farther, we find that the holiness movement grew out of Methodism, where we begin our study.

John Wesley and the Methodist church

John Wesley (1701–1791) was reared in Epworth, England. As a child he was deeply influenced by his mother, Susanna, who imposed on her children prescribed rules of conduct—"methods" of living. For this reason she has often been called the mother of the Methodist church.

John and his brother Charles became convinced that living by a set of definite rules and regulations was the way to improve oneself and to arrive at perfection. The two brothers were saddened by the cold, ritualistic atmosphere of the Anglican church and by the lack of spiritual life among its members. The Wesleys emphasized that perfection and holiness were indispensable to salvation and that exercising Christian virtue leads to perfection and holiness.

At Oxford University the Wesleys were members of the Holy Club, a fraternity whose members met to set their own spiritual lives in order. Their fellow students gave them the name Methodists to describe their methodical way of study and worship. John Wesley, however, still was not finding the peace for which he was searching. On Aldersgate Street at a Moravian group reading of Luther's preface to Romans, Wesley finally felt that he trusted in Christ alone for salvation and that his sins were taken away.

Wesley felt that the Aldersgate experience was a witness of the Holy Spirit that he had the necessary faith and strength to go on with a life of holiness. The deep emotional assurance that Christ was his Savior seems to have convinced Wesley that he was no longer subject to voluntary sins but was in possession of a constant and intense love for Christ. Wesley then felt capable of freeing himself from the wrath of God by living in holiness in the service of Christ and the world.

So Wesley's religious experience, rather than the objective promises of God, became the basis of his assurance of escape from the wrath of God. Later on, the holiness groups that sprang from Wesley's Methodism followed his example and emphasized individual religious experiences.

Wesley was Arminian in his theology. He taught that salvation is universal. He taught that there is a kingdom of the Father and another of the Holy Spirit. He held that people are responsible only for that which has been revealed to them, whether that be only the light of reason in the kingdom of the Father (in which everyone is a member) or an experiential knowledge of Christ (such as the experience Wesley had at Aldersgate) in the kingdom of the Spirit (in which people are expected to go on to perfection in their sanctification). Wesley thus taught that heathen people, even though they know nothing of Christ, will be saved if they make proper use of their reason, doing as much as their natural knowledge permits them to do.

Roots of Pentecostalism

In Wesley's doctrine of free salvation, fallen man is free to accept Christ or to reject him. Wesley taught that everyone possesses some measure of grace, which he called prevenient grace, that enables each person to make that decision. Wesley denied that people are totally corrupt by nature, in spite of the fact that they have lost God's original righteousness. He denied that people are completely without the divine image and totally dead in trespasses and sin. Therefore, since people have the ability to accept Christ, Wesley held that it ought to be possible to work them into the proper frame of mind by which they will finally consent to God's call. (This kind of thinking set the stage for long, drawn-out church meetings punctuated with emotional and enthusiastic hand clapping, singing, lively music, loud prayers, shouting, and strenuous urging of the sinner to accept Christ.)

Wesley taught full salvation. He taught a kingdom of the Holy Spirit and described the perfected man who belonged to that kingdom. Wesley's perfectionism is restricted only to those who have had an experiential knowledge of Christ and are thus in the kingdom of the Holy Spirit. This teaching contains the following four main points.

First, the essence of perfection is love. Second, the Christian is motivated by pure love and does not sin, *sin* being defined as "a willful transgression of a known law." This is also known as sinless perfection or entire sanctification. Wesley did not teach that man can attain absolute perfection in this life but only a relative perfection insofar as he is free from voluntary sin. All lust, greed, and hatred in the Christian is replaced with perfect love. The Christian who has perfect love may still make mistakes in judgment, and these mistakes require Christ's atonement. Yet, in effect, Wesley denied the constant struggle between the Christian's new, regenerate man and his sinful flesh, which Paul describes in Romans 7. Third, Christian perfection is both instantaneous and progressive. Fourth, in order to attain Christian perfection, a Christian must closely regulate this life. The lives of Wesley's followers were ordered by his prescribed discipline, which outlined every phase of the Christian life.

Wesley held that pure love, which is the essence of perfection, is attainable by the Christian at least at the moment of death, if not during life itself. He referred to this "still higher salvation" as immensely greater than that which a Christian received when he came to faith and found God's forgiveness. Wesley urged his followers to seek entire sanctification with all diligence, which they did—with an earnestness that sometimes became a fanatical zeal.

Wesley was also involved in mysticism. He sought mystical union with God in a life of joyful service to God and neighbor. Out of this type of mysticism, it seems, came his attitude toward the sacraments. He denied the regenerative power of Holy Baptism, since in his opinion God endowed people with spiritual gifts and these gifts, not the forgiveness attained in Baptism, united Christians with God. This teaching helped set the stage for the subjective and spontaneous experience of baptism in the Spirit, which has become the great distinguishing feature of the Pentecostal movement.

Early revivals in America

American religion in the 1700s and 1800s is noted for its revivals. Most notable are two "great awakenings," or periods of intense revival. The first great awakening began in 1734 under the leadership of Jonathan Edwards. Edwards was a Calvinist, a religion not generally associated with emotional outburst. His sermons, though lacking in those characteristics usually considered conducive to Pentecostal-type outbursts, nevertheless caused in his hearers "violent physical reactions expressing both fear and joy."[1]

This revival received a quickened pace under the leadership of George Whitefield, who conducted a six-week evangelistic campaign that turned a local awakening into one that affected all the colonies. Whitefield had been close friends with John Wesley in England and shared similar views about sanctification.

Methodism itself, which had spread throughout England during the 1700s, took root in America in 1766. Wesley sent Francis Asbury to the colonies to establish Methodism there. It took root in Virginia, where a revival took place from 1773 to 1776. But revival was followed by a period of deadness, and from that point on, the Methodists in America would experience the same cycle. Their leaders would continually return to Wesley's teaching of Christian perfection, entire sanctification, and the second blessing. Spurred on by Wesley, they would initiate periods of intense revival.

Early in the 19th century, Lyman Beecher began his preaching ministry in New England. He had a remarkable capacity for stirring up his audiences. About the same time, what has been termed the Kentucky revival spread the Methodist doctrine into Ohio and Pennsylvania. This revival was characterized by intense emotions and a wide variety of strange psychological and physical phenomena.[2] Participants experienced reactions such as falling, jerking, barking like dogs, falling into trances, and something called holy laughing. Characteristic of revival meetings and the camp meetings that grew out of them was fiery oratory by preachers and revivalistic laymen. They conducted meetings that were held night after night, often late into the night, followed by meetings with those who had been affected. The meetings were also characterized by prayer for the Holy Spirit.

Mention must be made of the revivalistic preacher Charles Finney of New York. From 1843 until his death, he stirred audiences with sermons that emphasized entire sanctification. Finney used the expression "baptism of the Holy Ghost" and generated the "powerful excitements" that he claimed the Holy Spirit must produce in people before leading them to obey God. That excitement, he claimed, must reach a pitch that produces a tide so high as to sweep away all opposing obstacles.[3]

Finney took the Methodist-type revival and gave it a unique style. He helped make revivalism the national religion of America. Finney was Arminian in theology. He denied the scriptural doctrine of original sin and taught instead that man has a free will. He also taught that conversion is man's choice and is accomplished by man's own personal surrender, hence the need for frenzied church meetings and emotional preaching. Finney, more than any other man, was responsible for formulating and popularizing the Methodist doctrine of entire sanctification during the 19th century. Finney exalted sanctification over justification.

Early holiness movements

In the middle of the 19th century, a general movement surfaced in the Methodist church that set the stage for modern Pentecostalism. There was an intense, renewed interest in Wesley's doctrine of entire sanctification and the second blessing.

This movement was a response to growing liberalism, formalism, and moral decay in the Methodist church. The same concerns that had been expressed in earlier revival movements were now shared by large numbers of Methodists. These Methodists formed holiness associations within the Methodist churches. Toward the end of the 19th century, up to half of all Methodists were part of this holiness movement.

Not all holiness groups, however, chose to remain in the Methodist church. Some started their own denominations. (The Church of the Nazarene is the largest of these.) Also, many of the more radical holiness followers felt they could remain faithful to God only by separating themselves from the Methodist church.

Inevitably, a rift grew within the Methodist church. Many within the church took a stand against the holiness movement. This led to the founding of many new holiness denominations. Twenty-three holiness groups were founded during the final decade of the 19th century.

What characterized the holiness movement was the emphasis on a *second* blessing, the baptism of the Holy Spirit that came on a person subsequent to his coming to faith. In 1895 a preacher named Benjamin Irwin began teaching a *third* blessing, the baptism of fire, which carried a person even beyond entire sanctification. Many in the holiness movement identified themselves with Irwin's Fire Baptized Holiness Church. After receiving the fire, they would often react with frenzied emotion, including shouting and speaking in tongues. Some would fall into a trancelike state. The more conservative holiness leaders disclaimed this third blessing of fire.

As the 19th century came to a close, advocates of the baptism of fire were still making noisy propaganda for their views, both from the pulpit and in print.

Putting it into perspective

In his exhaustive work *A Theology of the Holy Spirit*, Frederick Bruner summarizes the various forces at the end of the 19th century that converged to produce the Pentecostal movement: "Methodism was the modern soil upon which Pentecostalism flourished. Revivalism was in part and increasingly the American practice of Methodist theology, and Finney was the individual and the holiness movement the corporate vehicle of that theology and practice."[4] Bruner further states: "In Finney were combined both the theology (essentially Methodism) and the methodology (essentially revivalism) which were later to find a permanent home in the movement called Pentecostal."[5]

The main link between Methodism and Pentecostalism centers on the desire for spiritual experience, an experience that takes place following conversion. Methodism searched for an instantaneous experience of sanctification, while Pentecostalism aspired to an instantaneous Holy Spirit baptism subsequent to conversion.

The link between revival Methodism and Pentecostalism was forged by the holiness movement within the Methodist church. The search for the second blessing intensified as the 20th century drew near. The quest for the third blessing (and some even searched for yet higher blessings) was but a further intensification of the spirit of the times. The stage had been set for a new movement.

The beginning of the modern (classical) Pentecostal movement

Before we turn to what is generally considered the advent of modern Pentecostalism, we should point out that similar outbreaks of the spirit had already occurred in various parts of the United States and in other countries. (In the years before and shortly after the Azusa Street happenings in Los Angeles, California, which we will describe later in this chapter, outbreaks were noted that had no tie to Azusa Street.)

Pentecostal revivals flared up in New England as well as in North Carolina, Minnesota, Ohio, Georgia, and Florida. In 1904 during a great religious revival in Wales, tongues were heard amid Welsh singing.[6] In Mukti, India, some residents of a home for young widows and orphans, run by the well-educated Pandita Ramabai, began experiencing certain segments of what we are calling the baptism of fire. Some of the girls had formed evangelistic bands, and during a mission one of them began speaking in tongues. (This was in September 1906, the very month that the news of the Azusa Street revival arrived in India.)[7]

Some outbreaks in the United States spawned church bodies that had already organized when the Pentecostal movement began, and these church bodies served as ready receptacles of the Pentecostal spirit. We draw attention to one notable example. The oldest and third largest Pentecostal body in America is the Church of God, with headquarters in Cleveland, Tennessee. The Church of God grew from a small group formed in 1886 by Richard G. Spurling and his son, who held the same name. After the group prayed for revival, one finally broke out in Cherokee County, North Carolina, in 1896. The revival featured an extensive outburst of speaking in tongues.[8] This church body might be called the original Pentecostal denomination.

Terminology that later would be adopted by the Pentecostal movement was also being used at this time. Referring to Joel 2:23,28-32, many believed that the "former rain" of verse 23 (KJV) was a prophecy of the speaking in tongues that occurred in the early church, beginning on Pentecost Day. They interpreted the "latter rain" as a widespread bestowal of the gift of tongues on the church through an outpouring of the Holy Spirit that would occur at the end of the Christian era and just before the dawn of Christ's premillennial coming.[9] Pentecostals considered their speaking in tongues as the signal that Joel's prophecy was at last finding fulfillment and that the Christian era was indeed coming to an end.[10]

Parham, the father of modern Pentecostalism

The first major actor to appear on the stage set in the last decade of the 18th century was Charles F. Parham, the father of the modern Pentecostal movement.

Parham was a young Methodist minister in Topeka, Kansas, who was dissatisfied with his religious life and the power and success of his ministry. He felt that the Christians of the first century had a secret the church no longer shared. He believed that to find that secret would require much Bible study. Parham was impressed by the teachings of Frank Sanford, a restorationist (a person who believed in getting back to old-time New Testament Christianity) who in 1900 founded and operated a Bible school near Brunswick, Maine. Sanford's followers spoke of experiencing Spirit baptism.

In October 1900 Parham returned to Topeka and opened Bethel Bible College in order to continue his spiritual search. The school was established in a huge old mansion to which the townspeople had attached the descriptive name Stone's Folly, since its builder had run out of money before he could properly finish it. Parham charged no tuition but depended on each student to supply whatever he or she could. He was both director and student. Twelve of the 40 students at the college were ministers.

Just before Christmas 1900, Parham left the college for a few days. Before he left, he asked his students to search the Scriptures and try to find if there was a sign that would indicate if a person had received the Spirit. When he returned, all 40 of his students were in agreement: speaking in tongues was the sign.

The next day everyone in the old mansion joined Parham in a prayer to receive the baptism of the Holy Spirit along with the gift of speaking in tongues. The prayer began in the morning and continued all afternoon. Nothing happened, though there remained an air of expectancy among Parham and the students.

Agnes Ozman had been a Bible school student before coming to Parham's college. She felt a deep longing for an experience with the Holy Spirit. At about seven o'clock, Ozman recalled that some of the baptisms described in Acts were accompanied by the laying on of hands. She then requested Parham to place his hands on her head and pray for her to receive the baptism of the Holy Spirit.

At first he was reluctant to do so, but finally he acceded to her request. As soon as Parham laid his hands on her head, Ozman began to speak flowing syllables that neither she nor Parham could understand. This happened about 11 o'clock, one hour before the dawning of the new century (the significance of which has not been lost on Pentecostals). Parham claimed that Ozman spoke Chinese and that for three days she could not speak English.[11]

It is important to note that while there had been manifestations of tongues-speaking before this, especially in conjunction with evangelistic revivals, Ozman was the first person to speak in tongues after specifically seeking a baptism in the Holy Spirit and expecting to speak in tongues as a result.[12]

Over the next three days the group experienced many more Spirit baptisms, with tongues-speaking as evidence. On January 3, 1900, Parham and a dozen other ministers from various denominations gathered at Stone's Folly, and received the Spirit baptism.[13] Newspaper accounts of the tongues-speaking at the college brought many people to see and hear for themselves what was going on.[14] Before this, tongues-speaking had been associated with the emotional crisis of a revival meeting. But at Stone's Folly, it received a measure of respectability and began to be sought as a sign of the actual filling of the Holy Spirit and as the forerunner to the new life the Spirit brings.

Parham's initial dream to carry the Pentecostal revival across the United States and into Canada evaporated.[15] His group broke up and the college in Topeka closed when the old mansion was sold out from under the group. Parham moved the college to Kansas City, Kansas, where he found himself preaching on the street corners with no one listening. So he moved on to Lawrence, Kansas, where he began to hold services. In 1903 he again moved his operation, this time to El Dorado Springs, Missouri. In this resort town he found success in conducting free healing services. Later, at the invitation of a woman whom he had healed of an eye affliction, the revival preacher moved to Galena, Kansas. There the people welcomed Parham's Pentecostal, full gospel message of salvation, tongues-speaking, healing, and other gifts. Many experiences of tongues-speaking were reported there as Parham conducted his healing ministry. Parham later accepted an invitation to Orchard, Texas, where in two weeks he was successful in gaining almost the entire community to his full gospel message.

Parham met success in his revival meetings at Houston, Texas, and a number of other cities. In December 1905, he established a Bible school in Houston.[16]

By 1906, the year that Pentecostalism came to the Los Angeles area, Parham had more than eight thousand followers and was the principle Pentecostal leader. However, his influence waned after the outbreak on Azusa Street (which is described in the next section), and he died in virtual obscurity at Baxter Springs, Kansas. Furthermore, reports of Parham's sexual misconduct would not go away. These reports caused even his most faithful associates to reject his leadership and contributed to his waning popularity and influence.

Seymour and the Pentecostal explosion on Azusa Street

Among those who were attracted to Parham's Bible college in Houston, Texas, was a one-eyed, short, stocky, black holiness preacher named William J. Seymour. He became an ardent supporter of Parham's full gospel views.

A woman named Neeley Terry, while visiting from Los Angeles, attended Seymour's church in Houston and received the baptism of the Holy Spirit, which by this time had become a much publicized matter. Later, on returning to Los Angeles, she persuaded her home congregation, a Nazarene mission, to call Seymour to be the associate pastor. Seymour accepted the invitation and transferred his ministry to Los Angeles. Seymour's first sermon offended the people, especially his associate, Julia Hutchins. Even though they did not speak in tongues, the members of the congregation were convinced that they had already been baptized with the Spirit, which the Pentecostal preacher flatly denied in his sermon.

Later that day, when Seymour arrived at the church to conduct the afternoon service, he found the door bolted against his entry. This, however, did not stop him from preaching. At the invitation of a small group of Baptists, he began to conduct meetings in a private home.

On April 9, 1906, Pentecostalism "arrived" in California when seven people received the baptism of the Spirit and spoke in tongues. The sounds of the religious excitement taking place in the house attracted people on the streets. The word spread and attendance grew. At one especially tumultuous service, the old house in which Seymour preached literally collapsed when the floor gave way under the weight of the worshipers. No one was hurt, but the congregation was forced to move. It purchased an old Methodist church at 312 Azusa Street, and there the Apostolic Faith Gospel Mission found a home.

The building was kept open at all times and continually hummed with activity. Male and female preachers kept meetings going day and night for three years. At all hours people assembled for prayer in a large upstairs room. Many of them reportedly spoke in tongues and saw visions.[17]

The activities on Azusa Street attracted people from all over the country. The physical demonstrations they witnessed were often outlandish in nature. Some experienced the "jerks" and others "treed the devil" (they crawled around and barked like dogs to scare the devil away).[18] Many professed to have had a genuine spiritual experience. But many others were critical of the mission. Some suspected that demons, not the Holy Spirit, had taken control. Instead of scaring the devil away, Seymour seemed to attract him. Spiritualists and mediums from the numerous occult societies of Los Angeles joined the services and introduced séances and trances there.[19] All this disturbed Seymour a great deal, and he appealed to Parham for help. Parham, however, was unsuccessful in his attempts to wean the people away from their overemphasis on tongues-speaking and from their religious frenzy.[20] Visitors to the mission were increasingly repulsed by some of the goings-on between the sexes and races and by some of the singing.[21] Parham had a falling out with Seymour and denounced him, accusing him of being "possessed with a spirit of leadership." He denounced the mission as having come under the power of the "holy rollers and hypnotists" and their "awful fits and spasms."[22] Seymour himself did little preaching. Usually he was content to sit behind the pulpit, slouched over, with his head stuck in an old shoe box.

The spread of Pentecostalism

In spite of all this, the Azusa Street mission, with Seymour's three-year revival, attracted people from around the world and gave rise to the modern Pentecostal movement. People flocked to Azusa Street, hoping to meet God there.[23] When they returned to their homes, they took the Pentecostal revival with them. John L. Sherrill mentions that there were visitors from Chicago, Winnipeg, New York City, Little Rock, and even from London, Sunderland, Amsterdam, Oslo, Calcutta, Allagahad, and Mukti. The Pentecostal message needed no selling, but was instantly received.[24] Once the fires of modern Pentecostalism were lit, they spread until they were felt around the globe. In all, 26 church bodies trace their roots directly to the Azusa Street mission.

A good example of the spread of Pentecostalism is the story of Thomas Barratt, a Cornishman who pastored the Norwegian Methodist City Mission in Oslo, Norway. Barratt had come to the United States in 1905 to raise funds for his mission. He heard about the Pentecostal events in Los Angeles and received his baptism in the Spirit at a Pentecostal meeting in New York City. Barratt went on to spread Pentecostalism to Norway, England, Germany, and Sweden. He is called the father of the European Pentecostal movement.[25]

Links can be established between the US outbreak of Pentecostalism and those in China, Africa, and various Latin American countries. John Nichol, in his book *Pentecostalism,* tells how scores of immigrants, especially Italian and Persian, were affected by Pentecostalism at a Chicago mission. Some of the Persians returned to their homeland and preached there, while one of the Italians established small cells of Pentecostals throughout the United States. Later he worked in South America, while some of his colleagues returned to Italy and spread Pentecostalism in some of the major cities there.[26] The Pentecostal movement was exported from Chicago also to Brazil through immigrants who had adopted the message.[27]

About 1908 Pentecostalism and its accompanying phenomena appeared in China at the Wuchow schools, conducted by the Christian and Missionary Alliance. A number of people there began to speak in tongues. From Nichol's account, it does not seem as if the school officials were promoting it, but they did recognize it as similar to what they had heard was happening in Los Angeles. In a short period of time, 50 churches were added to the Pentecostal movement in China.[28]

Pentecostalism came to Central Africa somewhat later (1914–1915) via two Englishmen, and it spread through Tanganyika and Mozambique.[29]

Though unrelated, these groups all held in common the teaching that there is a need for a baptism in the Holy Spirit and the accompanying evidence of speaking in tongues.[30] In a few years, the term *Pentecostal movement* became common in referring to all such groups.[31]

It is beyond the scope of this book to list all the Pentecostal churches that were formed after 1906. We might trace the history in a general way as follows.

The years following the outbreak in Los Angeles saw a flurry of denominational organization and reorganization. First, recall that the seedbed of the Pentecostal outbreak was the holiness movement. Not all holiness bodies jumped at the Pentecostal spirit, however. One example is the Christian and Missionary Alliance, founded in 1887. While the Alliance emphasized sanctification and divine healing, it finally parted company with other Pentecostals on whether tongues-speaking is the sign of the second blessing. Can all Christians expect to speak in tongues? Is tongues-speaking the only sure sign that someone is filled with the Spirit? The Alliance answered both questions in the negative and simply said that a Christian should neither seek nor forbid speaking in tongues.[32] Its leader, Dr. A. B. Simpson, saw dangers in the tongues movement. He felt that its focus was too narrow and that it passed over other important gifts. He expressed the concern that counterfeit experiences may be ascribed to God and that undue interest in tongues would distract people from worshiping God. Simpson also took note of the divisions and controversies caused by the tongues movement.[33] Some holiness groups spoke with even stronger language, labeling the doctrine of Spirit baptism "third blessing heresy." Tongues-speaking was regarded by some as demon inspired. Some holiness groups dropped the term *Pentecostal* from their names.[34] The largest holiness group, the Church of the Nazarene, flatly denounces speaking in tongues but allows its members to decide for themselves on the matter of healing.

Second, some holiness groups adopted the Pentecostal spirit. We have already noted the case of the Church of God (Cleveland).[35]

Third, new Pentecostal church bodies formed, and during the subsequent years, serious attempts were made to unite the various Pentecostal groups.

Eventually the Assemblies of God (AOG) emerged as the largest single organization. Others include the Church of God in Christ, the United Pentecostal Church, the International Church of the Foursquare Gospel, and numerous smaller bodies.

In 1942 the AOG helped organize the National Association of Evangelicals (NAE) and in 1943 voted to affiliate with it. In May 1947 the first World Pentecostal Conference met in Zurich, Switzerland, and has met every three years since 1949. The Pentecostal Fellowship of North America (PFNA) was created in the late 1940s. Twenty-four Pentecostal denominations, including the AOG (since 1949), are members of this organization.[36]

The Full Gospel Business Men's Fellowship International

The Pentecostal movement has its share of parachurch organizations. One deserves special mention. The Full Gospel

Business Men's Fellowship International (FGBMFI) is a lay organization for Christian business men and women. It offers fellowship for those who have been baptized in the Holy Spirit and have spoken in tongues. Membership is also available to people from non-Pentecostal backgrounds, although the meetings feature Pentecostal-style worship and promote the full gospel (salvation plus the gifts of the Spirit). This organization, more than any other, has won members of the historic Christian churches for Pentecostalism.

FGBMFI has an interesting history. Its roots go back to the Armenian and Russian Pentecostalism that migrated to America about the turn of the 20th century. Its founder was Demos Shakarian, whose family led the Pentecostal movement in Armenia. He also served as international president of the FGBMFI. At age 13, Shakarian once spoke for four hours in other tongues after receiving what he claimed was the filling of the Holy Spirit. Later at home he collapsed helpless to the floor and heard what he thought to be the voice of God, asking him if he would ever again doubt his power.

In 1906 Shakarian happened across the Azusa Street mission, and these two existing "streams" of Pentecostalism met.[37] Shakarian later went into business, but his business failed in 1938. So he began to hold street meetings in a Los Angeles park. Later he went into business again and succeeded. With some of the proceeds, he began to sponsor evangelistic meetings and Pentecostal rallies. The revival of the gift of healing in Pentecostal meetings in the 1940s was the soil out of which the FGBMFI grew. With encouragement from Irvine J. Harrison and Oral Roberts, Shakarian attempted to found a businessmen's full gospel group. After a slow start, he received a prophecy through his wife and a vision that he concluded came from God, promising great success to his venture. Soon after that, he began to publish the magazine *Voice*, one of several popular FGBMFI publications. *Voice* is largely a collection of Pentecostal-type experiences of people from around the United States.

At FGBMFI meetings the members help those who have not spoken in tongues to receive the baptism in the Spirit and the tongues-speaking experience.

3

PENTECOSTALISM'S NEW FORCE:
THE CHARISMATIC MOVEMENT

The sudden rise and rapid spread of modern Pentecostalism at the beginning of the 20th century constitutes a religious drama so strange, so unusual, and so far-reaching that one could hardly look for a repeat performance. Nevertheless, that is what happened. In the 1950s once-cautious tongues-speakers came out in the open to tell of their experiences. Pentecostalism spilled over into Protestantism's mainline historic churches. In less than a decade, the present-day charismatic movement, or charismatic renewal, grew into a tidal wave that began sweeping the modern church. The charismatic movement, a religious phenomenon of the first order, claims the distinction of being the fastest growing and most extensive movement in history. During the past three decades, it has spread into every continent and major denomination.[1]

Reaction to the replaying of the Pentecostal drama in the mainline churches has ranged from total acceptance to total rejection. In many congregations it has simply been tolerated or even ignored. At times it has been accepted by theological communities that one would not have expected to be open to such things. Roman Catholicism is one exa mple; the Episcopal church, another. However, even in those bodies that have shown a somewhat friendly attitude toward the modern tongues-speaking movement, one does not find unanimity among the leaders in how they approach the issue. Nor is there unanimity among congregations or even among members of the same congregation. Millions of charismatics in both Protestant and Roman Catholic churches now claim to have experienced the old-line Pentecostal baptism in the Spirit.

It used to be said that Pentecostalism was attractive only to the naive and the gullible. The present charismatic movement, however, draws people from every walk of life. For example, *Trinity*, the first charismatic magazine, was produced by Jean Stone, the wife of a Lockheed Aircraft executive in Los Angeles. It made its debut as a slick-paper, sophisticated quarterly aimed at highbrows.[2] From the beginning, the charismatic renewal has appealed to professionals, intellectuals, and the sophisticated. Within a few years of its beginning, the charismatic movement included people from all walks of life in 40 denominations.[3] However, as we shall discover, the members of the charismatic renewal have often shown surprising gullibility when it comes to believing the claims of its leadership in matters of authority, prophecy, and healings.

As noted earlier, a big surprise is the overwhelming acceptance of the charismatic renewal by Roman Catholics. By 1980 Catholics in 120 countries were involved in the renewal. The claim is made that there are well over ten million American Catholics who have experienced the Pentecostal baptism in the Holy Spirit. This is a fact worth noting, especially when one considers that in the past the Roman Church has denounced tongues-speaking as demon produced, except when miraculous gifts of foreign languages were given and used on its foreign mission fields.

The beginning of the charismatic movement

No one seems to know exactly when the Pentecostal movement began to penetrate non-Pentecostal churches. It seems that for some time, many in the mainline churches had spoken in tongues, but in public they kept silent about it in order to avoid ridicule.[4] Mainline pastors were concerned about losing their pastorates should their Pentecostal experiences become known. In 1956 only about 20 pastors were open about their involvement in the charismatic movement.[5]

One thing is certain: the charismatic spirit came into the mainline churches through contacts their members had with classical Pentecostalism. An example of this is the experience of Harald Bredesen, a Dutch Reformed minister who traced his tongues-speaking experience to a Pentecostal camp meeting. Bredesen later brought the movement to Yale University.

From the beginning the Pentecostal movement had great influence on the charismatic movement and can even be regarded as a precipitating cause of it. At the same time, it must be recognized that the charismatic movement has done much to focus attention on Pentecostalism and even to promote it as a legitimate church movement. In fact, Pentecostalism was losing steam until the fervor of the charismatics caught on with the Pentecostals and stoked their fire.

It is not unreasonable to tie the beginnings of the charismatic movement to the work of the Full Gospel Business Men's Fellowship International. The FGBMFI began to attract other Christians to its gatherings, particularly to its prayer breakfasts and later to other conferences and programs. At their meetings the business men and women clap, sing, speak in tongues, and give testimonies. Guests from the historic churches are invited to join in, and not a few bow to the Pentecostal spirit.[6] Through the efforts of these converts, the word about Pentecostalism traveled across America. Testimonials began to surface among other Protestants and later among Roman Catholics.[7] Edward D. O'Connor of the University of Notre Dame, a leading charismatic Catholic, observes that most charismatic Catholics had their Pentecostal experience through the influence of a non-Catholic Pentecostal. He cites especially the influence of the FGBMFI.[8]

We might note that by 1980 the FGBMFI had 2,300 chapters in 27 countries and that the majority of its membership consisted of mainline Protestants and Roman Catholics.

The charismatic explosion: Father Dennis Bennett

Father Dennis Bennett's autobiography, *Nine o'Clock in the Morning,* tells the story of how Pentecostalism in the mainline churches came out of hiding and burst upon the scene on April 3, 1960. On that Sunday, Bennett, the rector of Saint Mark's Episcopal Church in Van Nuys, California, preached a sermon on the underground Pentecostal movement in America. He admitted his own experience of speaking in tongues. Bennett's confession touched off an immediate, violent reaction in the congregation. Rather than see his congregation suffer a split, the charismatic priest resigned his pastorate.

Bennett claimed that prior to his personal involvement, he was unaware of the charismatic movement. He also claimed that he had no theology of the Holy Spirit and that to him the Spirit was only a vague, theoretical being.

Bennett's involvement in the charismatic movement had begun when a young priest from a neighboring Episcopalian church informed Bennett of a young couple in his congregation who claimed to be baptized in the Holy Spirit and who spoke in tongues.[9] The couple had been at a prayer meeting in which they met a man who claimed the baptism in the Spirit. This man joined them in a prayer to receive the baptism, and they then experienced it.[10] Their church lives dramatically improved after their experience, and they began to tithe.[11]

Soon Bennett was introduced to the couple at its home. At first he wanted no part of tongues-speaking, but as time went on, he continued to be impressed by the joy and sincerity of the couple. Finally, convinced that the Scripture tells of baptism of the Spirit and of speaking in tongues and feeling an inner spiritual starvation, Bennett asked to receive the baptism in the Spirit and also to speak in tongues. The husband first prayed for him in tongues and then in English. He laid his hands on Bennett's head.[12] After Bennett himself prayed for about 20 minutes, his tongue "tripped," and he began to speak in a new language. At the time, he did not feel that his speaking in tongues was by psychological trick or from compulsion or that he had been carried away. He felt that he was in possession of his will.[13]

After a few days, Bennett went back to the couple's home and once again began to speak in tongues—"this time, after only about three or four minutes" in prayer.[14] Bennett spoke for about half an hour in tongues and found that except for forming the words, he had complete control of the language (speed, loudness, pitch, starting, and stopping).[15]

The first layperson in Bennett's church to speak in tongues was a lady, a hard worker for the congregation. Depressed about her spiritual state, she had come to see Bennett, her priest. He responded by telling her of his new experience. She felt greatly uplifted and later began to speak in tongues, the first of many in the congregation to do so.[16] The number of those who received the baptism grew, not only at Bennett's church but also in the congregation of Bennett's friend, where it had all started with the one charismatic couple.

At one meeting attended by 14 charismatic Episcopalians and others, a young priest who entertained a wait-and-see attitude prayed for a while and then received Spirit baptism. He jumped to his feet and began to speak very rapidly in tongues.[17]

Although she greatly desired it, Bennett's wife was slow to get the gift of tongues. One night she knelt beside her bed and told the Lord she would not get up until she received the gift of tongues. She fell asleep and then later awoke speaking in a new tongue.[18] Bennett's children, together with other youngsters in the congregation, also began speaking in tongues.[19]

A few healings had occurred at Saint Mark's even before Bennett and others received their baptism in the Spirit. But afterwards, healings were far more frequent.[20] Giving also increased. Bennett discovered at one point that the 60 people who had received the baptism and were members of the prayer fellowship group were supporting ten percent of the budget in a church in which the membership was so large it required the care of four pastors.[21]

It is interesting to note that when he began to speak in tongues, Bennett did not accept the Scriptures in their entirety as the work of the Holy Spirit. But as he continued in the "life of the Spirit," he claimed he was compelled to accept the Scripture as the work of the Spirit.[22]

Speaking in tongues, which came to mean so much to the priest and other members, became a divisive force in the congregation. Silence on Bennett's part only fueled the fires of discontent.[23] Thus things really began to fall apart on April 3, 1960, when Bennett took to the pulpit and spoke about his charismatic experience. The situation dramatically worsened after the second service, when an assistant tore off his vestments, threw them on the altar, and said he could no longer work with Bennett. People who had spoken in tongues came forward to give their testimonies to others in the parish, while the opposition felt that Bennett should resign.[24]

By the third morning service, Bennett was convinced that resigning his position was the thing to do, lest the church go through a long, painful ordeal and much adverse publicity. Yet the announcing of his resignation during the service brought the whole charismatic movement out of hiding and into the public eye. Bennett's resignation caught the attention of the press. The priest was interviewed on the Paul Coates news program of KTTV, Los Angeles, and upon request spoke in tongues. Later, *Newsweek* featured an article on Bennett and his charismatic group.[25] Still later, *Time* did a feature on him.[26]

The prayer groups in which participants had spoken in tongues separated from Saint Mark's and continued under the name Holy Spirit Fellowship. Jean Stone, who had been a member of Saint Mark's and had received the baptism, founded the quarterly *Trinity*, a charismatic magazine slanted to the theology of the Episcopal church. She and others went on to spread the charismatic message. Stone took to the lecture circuit, her key message being that the baptism in the Spirit is for every Christian.[27]

In the meantime, Bennett was offered Saint Luke's, a small Episcopal parish in Ballard, Washington. The Episcopal bishop of Olympia, William Fisher Lewis, was open-minded on tongues, so Bennett gladly accepted the challenge to serve this almost defunct congregation in the heart of Seattle.

Back in Los Angeles, Bishop Bloy banned "the use of tongues under church auspices,"[28] while Bishop Pike in San Francisco called tongues-speaking a heresy in embryo. Bennett's successor at Saint Mark's placed a notice in his weekly newsletter in which he termed the practice of speaking in tongues "divisive." He went on to warn that it often led to overzealous claims for power.[29] Still, in spite of this early opposition by clergy to the charismatic renewal, by 1984, 47% of the world's Anglican bishops had openly identified with it.

Soon, Saint Luke's in Seattle began to repeat the recent history of Saint Mark's in Van Nuys. Only at Saint Luke's, most of the congregation was receptive to Spirit baptism.[30] Healings also began to take place at the church.[31] Bennett's bishops in Seattle backed him in his charismatic renewal venture.[32] As a result of Bennett's work, other Episcopalian priests were receiving the baptism in the Spirit and the gift of speaking in tongues.

As time went on, Bennett concluded that the main thrust of his work was to carry the Pentecostal message to church leaders and groups worldwide. His congregation concurred. The speed and ease with which the ubiquitous Bennett brought charismatic renewal to individuals, groups, and churches—whether in California, Washington, Alaska, or England—is nothing short of amazing. He left a multitude of tongues-speaking Pentecostals in his wake. At one meeting in England, 70 people received the baptism in the Spirit simultaneously and began to speak in tongues.[33]

Bennett's work was not confined to the Episcopal church. His lectures took him to religious leaders and groups across the theological spectrum, a practice not unusual for those stumping the charismatic trail. His Sunday services and charismatic prayer meetings attracted many people from other denominations. These people were urged to go back and work within their own groups to spread the Pentecostal message.

Reverend Herbert Mjorud, an evangelism official of the American Lutheran Church (now a part of the Evangelical Lutheran Church in America [ELCA]), published his personal experience at Bennett's Holy Spirit fellowship meetings. The meeting he attended was not what he had expected. Instead of boisterous ecstatic activity, he found in the service a quiet and orderly atmosphere. Bennett spoke for nearly two hours, followed by a coffee break. Then came a time of prayer and praise during which only the members of Saint Luke's were allowed to take part in evidencing charismatic gifts. This was done to ensure good order. During the prayer and praise time, Mjorud heard someone speak in an unknown tongue, after which another person spoke an interpretation in English. This procedure was followed several times. The second tongues-speaker reportedly spoke in Mandarin Chinese. A Chinese Christian in the audience agreed that the message had been given in Chinese and that it had been correctly interpreted.

After Bennett left for the evening, 70 to 80 charismatic members of Saint Luke's stayed to counsel the visitors. Mjorud was approached by a young man who offered to help him. When Mjorud introduced himself as an evangelist, he was then asked if he had received the baptism of the Spirit and if he spoke in tongues. Finally, Mjorud asked the evangelist to pray with him. They knelt down by a pew at the rear of the church. After some persuasion on the part of the counselor, Mjorud agreed to have the counselor pray that Mjorud might receive all the gifts of the Spirit, including the gift of tongues. The counselor assured him that he could now speak in other tongues. Though Mjorud opened his mouth and tried, not a single sound came out. By this time, two other young men had joined them, and all three began to encourage him to speak in another tongue. The men kept on and on with their exhortations and prayers, both in English and in tongues. Mjorud was exhorted to *claim* the gift of tongues in Jesus' name, but still nothing happened. Once again the trio laid hands on Mjorud, asking God to deliver his mind from all reservations and inhibitions. Finally Mjorud decided to end the counseling session, pointing out that they had prayed for hours and that it seemed as if it wasn't his time. His counselors agreed.

Mjorud said he experienced a burning, or electrical, feeling in his head where they had laid hands on him. This, he felt, assured him he had received the baptism in the Spirit. Weeks later, when Mjorud deliberately attempted to speak in tongues, he succeeded. But he also told of doubts he had after the novelty of the gift of tongues had worn off.[34]

Bennett became a recognized world leader of the charismatic movement. His wife became his coworker, and together they spread the story of Holy Spirit renewal. As author, lecturer, world-traveler, and TV personality, Bennett, more than any other individual, gave the modern tongues movement shape and form. This is especially true within his own denomination, which has proven to be a fertile ground for the seeds of Pentecostalism. In fact, the impact of the charismatic renewal within the Episcopal church became strong enough to foster a mutual conference with the Assemblies of God for the purpose of discussing the ministry of the Holy Spirit in modern times.[35]

Lutherans join in

Of Protestant denominations, the Lutherans are second only to the Episcopalians in being open to charismatic renewal. At about the same time Bennett was receiving his baptism of the Spirit, Larry Christenson, a San Pedro pastor and a member at that time of the American Lutheran Church, attended a service in a Foursquare Gospel church. That night he awoke to hear himself speaking in tongues. Later, Allen Hansen, a Lutheran pastor in the Los Angeles area, also spoke in tongues. The two pastors received the support of Mjorud, the evangelism official of the American Lutheran Church who, as we just described, had been exposed to the charismatic movement at one of Bennett's prayer meetings in Seattle.

The controversy surrounding the Lutheran pastors helped bring the charismatic movement to the attention of the Christian world.[36] In an article in the *Lutheran Charismatic Newsletter,* entitled "Lutherans—the 'Man in the Middle,'" Christenson, a long-time leader of the renewal, points back to 1970, when Lutheran charismatics were just beginning to find one another. He characterizes the renewal among Lutherans as an underground criss-cross of personal contacts. No one knew how many others shared the same experience. But in 1972 Norris Wogen, a Lutheran pastor from

Iowa, suggested that the International Lutheran Conference on the Holy Spirit convene in Minneapolis, Minnesota. When ten thousand people attended, many were caught by surprise. It should be noted, though, that among the group were a large number of non-Lutherans.

Attendance at the conference grew to about 15,000 the next year, 1973. By 1976 it had grown to 25,000. The International Lutheran Conference on the Holy Spirit became an annual event that continued to be held into the 1990s. National Leaders' Conferences for Lutheran charismatic renewal were convened in 1974 and 1975, bringing together a cross section of pastors and laity serving both within official Lutheran structures and in independent ministries.

Lutheran Charismatic Renewal Services was organized to sponsor the annual International Lutheran Conference on the Holy Spirit, to assist in setting up local and regional conferences, and to produce literature and tapes. It also strove to maintain contacts with mainline Lutheran officials on behalf of Lutherans in charismatic renewal. Its leadership represented a fair cross section of the renewal among Lutherans.[37] Later, Lutheran Charismatic Renewal Services merged with the International Lutheran Center for Church Renewal to form the International Lutheran Renewal Center, with Christenson as director. This group represents pastors from the largest Lutheran bodies in the United States (the Wisconsin Evangelical Lutheran Synod is not included).

In his book *Charismatic Renewal Among Lutherans,* Christenson gives a bit of the early history of Lutheran charismatic renewal. He reports that in the summer and fall of 1961, small, scattered groups of Lutherans around the United States began to have the charismatic experience. Included in the experience, which focuses on the reality and power of the Holy Spirit in the Christian's life, was the receipt of such spiritual gifts as tongues-speaking, prophecy, and healing. At the beginning there appeared to be a simultaneous outbreak of charismatic activity in California, Minnesota, and Montana.[38]

The renewal spread to certain Lutheran groups in Germany and then to Lutherans in Scandinavia, Eastern Europe, Africa, Asia, Australia, and South America. Christenson points out that within 12 years practically every segment of the worldwide Lutheran church had been touched by the charismatic renewal.

By 1963 tongues-speaking had already taken such a firm hold on various Protestant pastors and laypeople that the American Lutheran Church ordered a special committee to study it. The committee's report neither approved nor condemned the practice but pointed out that "there is a danger of over-emphasis on glossolalia (speaking in tongues) on the part of some, with a distorted Christian perspective as the outcome."[39]

In 1972 the Lutheran Church—Missouri Synod's Commission on Theology and Church Relations issued a report titled "The Charismatic Movement and Lutheran Theology." The report contains this warning: "The Church must not conclude that because the Christian community in apostolic times had members who could speak in tongues, therefore the Church today must possess similar gifts or it is somehow incomplete. . . . The Church should seek the Holy Spirit and his gifts where God has promised them, in the Word and Sacraments. . . . Word and Sacraments are the instruments of the Spirit of God through which God continues to give his gifts to the Church in this and every age."[40] As of the date of this book, it is estimated that more than four hundred pastors of the Lutheran Church—Missouri Synod (LCMS) are involved in the charismatic movement.

From December 1984 to September 1986, representatives of the LCMS and charismatic pastors of the LCMS held three meetings. The charismatic pastors took exception to the 1977 synodical resolution "To Clarify the Synod's Position Regarding Charismatic Teaching." This resolution was adopted in response . . .

> . . . to the claim on the part of some individuals and groups within the charismatic movement that God has promised and does in fact give guidance and leadership to the church today through visions and dreams or direct prophecy. The synodical representatives emphasized that this resolution clearly states that such a claim must be regarded as a mere human opinion and that to elevate such human opinion to

> the level of Scriptural doctrine is contrary to the Scriptures and therefore dangerous to the salvation of people. The charismatic pastors on the other hand, stated it is also dangerous to salvation to say that the Scriptures teach that these gifts have definitely ceased today.[41]

The charismatic pastors expressed the concern that the LCMS position calls into question the experiences of the charismatic renewal and considers them contrary to the Scriptures. The fear was expressed by the charismatics that unless something is done to clarify the LCMS position in this matter, large numbers of charismatics would leave the LCMS.

Renewal in Missouri (RIM), the name adopted by LCMS charismatics, traces back to the three meetings mentioned. These were some of the questions frequently asked of the charismatic pastors: Who speaks for such a varied movement and how can they relate to it? What do LCMS charismatics really believe? (They seem to hold a wide range of positions.) Besides as an attempt to answer these questions, RIM was formed to assist the LCMS with serious theological study that would present something of a common understanding relative to this renewal movement.

The 53 founders and associates of RIM decided to become "vulnerably visible" as they attempted to bring a "balanced word" relative to the Holy Spirit and his gifts to the LCMS. They said: "It is our view that the majority of the Synod has mostly heard only warnings and negative input relative to these matters. Since renewal is more than spiritual gifts, we are focusing major attention in working together in our Synod to foster *bold witness, dynamic worship, and vibrant faith. . . .* We are currently publishing our quarterly RIM newsletter, *RIM Report*, which is mailed to every pastor in the Missouri Synod and Lutheran Church—Canada."[42] RIM has held national gatherings in 1988 and 1990, conducted 12 districtwide pastor's renewal seminars, and held several regional conferences.

Over the years there has been a marked defection by Lutheran charismatics from their respective bodies. Christenson leads us to believe that many Lutherans in the United States who are involved in the charismatic renewal have all but given up on the Lutheran church as such. He makes the further observation that this attitude is most pronounced among charismatics in the ELCA. The spiritual malaise in the ELCA has caused a significant number of charismatics to leave the Lutheran church and join Pentecostal or nondenominational churches. Christenson concludes that Lutheran charismatics feel betrayed and alienated from their churches when they see in church leaders what they perceive to be a massive defection from biblical theology and morality. He sees among ELCA members a lack of a sense of love, even of regard, for the Lutheran church.[43]

Popularity among Protestants

Both the United Presbyterian Church and the Southern Presbyterian Church found it necessary to appoint committees to study the charismatic renewal. The committee of the United Presbyterian Church published its "Report of the Special Committee on the Work of the Holy Spirit," which approved present-day tongues-speaking. However, the committee did caution that undue emphasis should not be placed on tongues and that the normal sphere of tongues-speaking is private worship. The committee also set up pastoral guidelines for directing the charismatic movement, with the hope of heading off the formation of cliques.[44]

The committee also cautioned against the teaching that tongues-speaking is the sole evidence of reception of the Holy Spirit:

> To insist that speaking in tongues is a necessary proof that one has been baptized by the Spirit is to overlook the clear statement of the apostle in 1 Corinthians 12:13, "For by one Spirit we were all baptized into one body [the Church]." Since only some of the Corinthian believers spoke in tongues (1 Corinthians 12:8-10), yet all of them (as Paul here specifically declares) have been baptized by the Spirit, it is unwarranted to teach that speaking in tongues is an indispensable sign of having received the Spirit.[45]

In the 1960s and 1970s, the charismatic movement made deep inroads into churches across the theological spectrum.

The best evidence is the popularity of Pentecostal meetings such as the charismatic convention that was held at the Kansas City Chiefs' football stadium in 1977. It is reported that some 50,000 charismatics—Roman Catholics, Lutherans, Baptists, Episcopalians, Mennonites, Presbyterians, Methodists, and nondenominational Christians—came together under the theme "Unity in the Lordship of Jesus." Messianic Jews were also listed among the participants.

Not all Protestant bodies have extended a welcome to the charismatic renewal. The Protestant Reformed Church's reaction to it has been bluntly negative. The foreword to the third printing of *Try the Spirits: A Reformed Look at Pentecostalism,* by Professor David J. Engelsma, published under the auspices of the evangelism committee of the Protestant Reformed Church, states:

> By this time, it is evident to all that the charismatic movement (or, neo-Pentecostalism) is no vagrant breeze wafting through the Protestant churches, but a mighty wind blowing steadily in these churches. Nor does this surprise us. Religion, like nature, abhors a vacuum. Bereft these many years of solid doctrine, expository preaching and thorough doctrinal instruction, the churches are exposed to the inrushing stream of mysticism. Starved of the "strong meat" of the Word (Hebrews 5:12-14), the empty souls of the members of these churches crave the insubstantial air of feeling. Although the powerful presence of the charismatic wind in the Protestant churches does not surprise us, it does grieve us. We call our fellow Protestants, especially all Reformed Christians, to resist the neo-Pentecostal hurricane: "be no more children, tossed to and fro, and carried about with every wind of doctrine" (Ephesians 4:14). By the infallible rule of Holy Scripture, "try the spirits whether they are of God" (1 John 4:1).[46]

Moreover, Engelsma states in his pamphlet:

> The wonders of Pentecostalism, like the miracles of Rome, are fraudulent.They are part and parcel of the only miracles that Scripture prophesies for the last days: the signs and wonders of the false christs and false prophets who would deceive the very elect, if it were possible (Matthew 24:24);

the power and signs and lying wonders of the man of sin who will deceive those who do not receive the love of the truth (2 Thessalonians 2:9-12).[47]

Tongues-speaking on campus

In 1962 a small group of students—members of the Yale Christian Fellowship—spoke in tongues while meeting with the charismatic pastor Harald Bredesen of a Reformed church in New York State. He had been recommended to the Fellowship by the editor of *Trinity*. Several spoke in tongues. Later the same night, several others emulated the experience. A Yale faculty member who had entered the meeting out of curiosity later also spoke in tongues.[48]

From Yale the charismatic renewal spread to Dartmouth, Princeton, and other universities across the nation.[49] Very early in the history of the charismatic movement, institutions of higher learning of various sorts were involved. This in itself was a new twist for Pentecostalism, since historically it had not been closely allied with higher education.

Roman Catholic charismatic renewal

Perhaps the greatest surprises in connection with the renewal were its acceptance by many Roman Catholics and the openness with which it was received by members of the Catholic hierarchy. Pentecostalism entered the Catholic Church through its universities, beginning with Duquesne, in Pittsburgh. According to Kevin and Dorothy Ranaghan in *Catholic Pentecostals*, the charismatic renewal came to Duquesne as the result of a corporate longing on the part of certain faculty members for a more dynamic Christian life. In fall 1966 these laypeople involved themselves in a series of prayer-discussion meetings during which they asked the Holy Spirit to renew in them all the graces of their baptisms and confirmations and to fill them with the powerful life of the risen Christ. They also began to study especially the history of the church presented in the New Testament. The more they studied, the more they began to expect the Holy Spirit to come to them. Each day they prayed for a divine visitation.[50] In August 1966, the group was introduced to the story of

David Wilkerson in *The Cross and the Switchblade.*[51] It led them to examine carefully the teachings concerning the Holy Spirit baptism.[52]

The account of the tongues movement by Sherrill, *They Speak with Other Tongues,* brought it all to a head. The group felt the time had finally come to act on all the praying they had done to receive the Spirit. They agreed to find someone who had actually received the baptism in the Spirit. William Lewis, rector of a large Episcopal congregation in Pittsburgh, put them in contact with one of his lady parishioners who was a permanent member of a Pentecostal prayer group. This lady invited them to a prayer meeting the following week. There they were exposed to a "lengthy spontaneous prayer session," during which they heard praying in tongues for the first time.[53] Two of the four who attended were convinced that what they had seen was a movement of God, so they attended the next meeting. At the end, the two asked that the group pray that they receive the baptism in the Holy Spirit. One of them, Ralph Keifer, told of being asked to "make an act of faith for the power of the Spirit to work in [him]."[54] After that, he prayed in tongues. He described it as not being a "soaring or spectacular" experience but a peaceful one.[55] In the following week, the remaining two of the four received the baptism in the Spirit after Keifer laid hands on them.[56]

Those who received the baptism felt they had experienced inner transformation. It was reported that they received many or all of the gifts of the Holy Spirit detailed in 1 Corinthians 12.[57]

The original four faculty members who had pursued the baptism of the Holy Spirit had all received it by February 1967. They began a quiet program of witnessing to close friends about their Pentecostal experience and what it had done for them. In the middle of that February, one of the most remarkable incidents in the Pentecostal movement took place. On what has been called Duquesne weekend, a small group of students met with the faculty members for a weekend retreat to pray and to study Acts 1 to 4. Most of the students came to the retreat having read David Wilkerson's story in *The Cross and the Switchblade* but knowing little or nothing of Holy

Spirit baptism. The group prayed and studied all day Saturday, and by evening the people had grown weary of their religious exercises. However, during their evening of relaxation, they experienced an overwhelming series of spontaneous charismatic occurrences. They experienced what they felt was the Holy Spirit being poured out on them. Some spoke in tongues. Some displayed other reactions. Prayer was held from ten in the evening until five the next morning.[58]

The Catholic charismatic renewal spread outward from Duquesne to other universities, such as Notre Dame, Michigan State, Iowa State, and Holy Cross in Worchester, Massachusetts. From the beginning, the Catholic intellectual community and socially elite were involved. Guidance was furnished by theologians such as Father Edward O'Connor, Father Francis McNutt, and Monsignors Ralph Keifer and Kevin Ranaghan.

The renewal spread in an ever-widening circle beyond the universities to parishes, convents, and monasteries.[59] Soon it encompassed all age groups and social strata. Ten years after Duquesne weekend, an estimated two million Catholics in the United States were involved in the renewal. By 1997 that figure was estimated to be around ten million.

By now, any hostility of the Roman Catholic Church toward the Pentecostal Church has disappeared. Qualified approval was given to the Catholic charismatic renewal by Cardinal Leo Josef Suenens of Belgium, whom Catholics regard as a "powerful prince of the Church."[60] A featured speaker at the Seventh Renewal Conference at Notre Dame, Suenens made it clear that he had come to give his enthusiastic approval to the movement within the Catholic Church. He is quoted as saying: "The charismatic renewal has extraordinary ecumenical implications. . . . Many important breakthroughs are happening in a wonderful way in the charismatic renewal. It will be a great impetus for Christian unity."[61] Suenens' words were prophetic, for the Church of Rome, with the blessing of Pope John Paul II, has made great use of the renewal in its ecumenical thrust to the Protestants. In an interview granted to Ralph Martin at Ann Arbor, Michigan, Suenens had this to say:

We can't say the gift of tongues is impossible or that it's crazy or doesn't make sense. It is clearly described in scripture as something that God gives, that has value. Secondly, the caution that Scripture expresses about tongues is that it should be expressed in an orderly way, not that it should be prohibited or that it is valueless. . . . I also get a glimpse of an additional meaning: God is being glorified in all the tongues of the world. . . . But in the end we must simply say that this is another of those "surprises of the Holy Spirit"— another instance where God chooses to work in a way that we humans would never have anticipated or chosen.[62]

O'Connor, associate professor of theology at Notre Dame, concludes that the Catholic charismatic movement is an extension of the Pentecostal movement that began in Topeka.[63] He believes that the Pentecostal movement, in spite of its origins, does not discredit "the institutional Church" (Roman Catholicism), but gives it new life and a deeper appreciation of liturgy, traditions, and sacraments.[64]

On the other hand, there are those who challenge the validity of the Pentecostal movement because it is a movement that originated outside the one "fully authentic" church and then entered it. In the minds of many Catholics, this raises a question as to proper order. If the Catholic Church is *the* church and if the charismatic renewal is a movement that has blessings from the Holy Spirit for the Catholic Church, why, then, did it not arise within Catholicism?

In spite of the objections, the attitude of the Catholic Church is not to condemn the charismatic renewal but to recognize its right to exist and to judge it by the spiritual-looking fruit it produces in those who participate. All that Rome requires is the involvement of priests to help safeguard the church's doctrine from being replaced by a theology of experience.[65] The "Statement of the Theological Basis of the Catholic Charismatic Renewal" offers the following advice: "This charism, whose existence in the New Testament communities and in the early post-apostolic times is well attested, should neither be given undue attention nor despised."[66]

One of the truly amazing aspects of the Roman Catholic charismatic renewal has been the willingness of church leaders to carry on ecumenical fellowship with non-Catholic charismatics and now also with people in the classical Pentecostal movement. Among the 20,000 charismatics who attended the fourth International Lutheran Conference on the Holy Spirit in Minneapolis, about one-third of the total were not Lutheran. Most of these were Catholic charismatics.

A striking example of Rome's attitude toward the movement occurred when Pope John Paul II addressed some 523 delegates of the world's charismatic renewal movement at the fourth International Conference of Charismatic Leaders in Rome. He told them: "Your choice of Rome as the site of this conference is a special sign of your understanding of the importance of being rooted in that Catholic unity of faith and charity which finds its visible center in the See of Peter."[67] He went on to give the renewal some guidelines:

> The first of these principles is fidelity to the authentic doctrine of the faith. Whatever contradicts this doctrine does not come from the Spirit. Secondly, you must be concerned to provide solid food for spiritual nourishment through the breaking of bread of true doctrine. Thirdly, as leaders in the renewal, you must take the initiative in building bonds of trust and cooperation with the bishops. Finally, by your experience of many gifts of the Holy Spirit, which are shared also with our separated brothers and sisters, yours is the special joy of growing in a desire for the unity to which the Spirit guides us and in a commitment to the serious task of ecumenism.[68]

Charismatic Ralph Martin, who was attending the conference, responded to the pope's words with the following affirmation of charismatic solidarity with the See of Peter: "On behalf of all of us here and all those in the charismatic renewal from all over the world, I want to pledge to you our loyalty and our love, and to let you know that our prayer groups and our communities in our parishes and our dioceses, are at your service." As a traditional sign of faithfulness on behalf of the delegates, Martin knelt and kissed the papal ring.[69]

The charismatic's goal: denominational renewal

Christians in the charismatic renewal now find that they have in common an experience that transcends theological traditions, historical boundaries, and ecclesiastical customs. The conference on charismatic renewal in the Christian churches held in 1977 at Kansas City was an outgrowth of the widespread desire among charismatics from many different denominations to demonstrate unity in the Spirit. Some observers feared that the movement itself would degenerate into a carbon copy of a denominational group. In the early 1970s, some leaders urged that charismatics ought to separate from their denominations. They even branded denominationalism as an evil. Some charismatic leaders were even rebaptizing denominational charismatics and urging them to separate from their groups.[70] They felt that the common experience of baptism in the Spirit was sufficient reason for all charismatics to come together for fellowship, joint prayer and praise, and mutual strengthening. In the process they would purge old denominational hostilities.

What finally prevailed was an attitude of harmony; charismatic leaders urged their followers to stay in their own denominations and to work for the renewal *of the group*. They were aware that the charismatic renewal needed the stability and the protection of the institutional church.[71] So now fellowship among charismatics is supplied by ecumenical prayer groups, conferences, and conclaves. These provide the opportunity to emphasize the unity they feel they possess in the Holy Spirit.

An example of this is provided by a Lutheran pastor and tongues-speaker who wrote in the Full Gospel Business Men's Fellowship International *Voice:*

> I have been having dialogues with Catholics and Pentecostals and it has been a wonderful blessing. In Brooklyn we have two dialogue groups now, composed of Lutheran ministers of all flavors and young Roman Catholic priests. We meet and study the Scriptures together, pray together, talk about community problems, and discuss mutual involvement of our parishes. Recently I attended a Roman Catholic, Episcopalian, and Lutheran retreat. The Holy Spirit is

moving in the Roman Catholic Church. I am convinced that the basic meaning of the Charismatic Renewal is the reunion of the churches. Not a reunion of compromise, or the creation of a super-church, but a renovation as to what the unity of the Spirit means.[72]

Some in the charismatic movement are looking forward to what they call the third wave of renewal. The first wave is classical Pentecostalism. The second wave is neo-Pentecostalism, or the charismatic renewal. Reverend Philip Gehlhar, writing in *RIM Report* (a newsletter published by LCMS charismatics), says:

The third wave, according to David Barrett, are the thousands of churches and pastors who want renewal in their churches, but do not want to think of themselves as charismatic. They have a heart for ministry and believe in the power of prayer for healing as well as for other needs. They want their worship services to be dynamic and reach people to inspire them and meet their needs. They want to see the church grow and bring people around the globe into a saving relationship with Jesus Christ.[73]

RIM also wants to include those in its ministry; we want to help pastors and congregations grow in every way into Christ. While we do not rule out or exclude any work as a gift of the Spirit, we do not reject or exclude any one simply because he or she has not received specific 'charismatic gifts.' Perhaps you never identified with the word 'charismatic.' Yet you do want to be open to receive and follow the leading of the Holy Spirit. Perhaps you seek to manifest stronger leadership in your church, or to find ways to get on with important things of God instead of petty bickering. RIM invites you to contact us and we will seek to be of help.[74]

It remains to be seen how well such reaching out by charismatics to the so-called third wave is received.

Part Two

THE TEACHINGS AND PRACTICES

OF THE

PENTECOSTAL/CHARISMATIC

MOVEMENT

4

HOLY SPIRIT BAPTISM

Pentecostals/charismatics notice the lack of power in today's church but see the evidence of power in the early church; they want that power. They feel that the present church neglects the Holy Spirit, whereas the early church emphasizes the Spirit. They fear that the present church has the Holy Spirit too much as a *doctrine*, whereas the early church had the Spirit as an *experience*. The heart of Pentecostal/charismatic religious life is an experience termed "baptism in or with the Holy Spirit." This experience convinces the Christian that he is the object of the Holy Spirit's concern and that he is ordained by the Spirit for service and mission in the world.[1]

Baptism in the Spirit

Holy Spirit baptism is the reason the Pentecostal/charismatic movement exists. Simply stated, it is the teaching (verified by one's experience) that subsequent to conversion there is available to the Christian who seeks it a *power* from Christ through the Holy Spirit. To receive that power is to receive the Holy Spirit.[2] Pentecostals/charismatics believe that, up to the time of Holy Spirit baptism, the Christian has only an indefinite relationship with the Spirit but that this becomes definite through the Pentecostal experience. In his Spirit baptism, the Christian receives the Holy Spirit, who thereafter permanently and personally comes to dwell in him. Before this personal indwelling, the Spirit merely reveals, or imparts, another person (that is, Christ), but in Spirit baptism the Holy Spirit imparts himself. God and man meet in man. By imparting his gifts to the Christian, the invisible Spirit becomes visible in the Christian. For the Pentecostal or charismatic, the object is to have the Spirit not just as an external instrument, but for internal enjoyment. Finally, from the moment of his Spirit baptism, the Christian does not enjoy only a partial experience of the Spirit, who influences him sporadically, but a full experience.[3] In the words of one astute observer, Pastor Joel Gerlach:

> Pentecostals believe that the Holy Spirit is to be received twice, once in conversion and again in Spirit baptism. In conversion a Christian merely receives the Spirit; in Spirit baptism he fully receives the Spirit and is empowered thereby for service in the church. . . . Every Christian has been baptized by the Spirit into Christ, but not every Christian has been baptized by Christ into the Spirit.[4]

To put it another way, in conversion the Holy Spirit-as-agent uses the atoning blood of Christ-as-means to bring about baptism into Christ, the new (spiritual) birth. But in Holy Spirit baptism, Christ-as-agent uses the Holy Spirit-as-element to baptize the Christian in or with the Holy Spirit to endue the Christian with power.[5]

There are three major points, then, in the Pentecostal doctrine of Holy Spirit baptism. First, although every believer at his conversion receives the Holy Spirit to some extent, he receives the Holy Spirit fully, in a permanent and personal way, at the time he is baptized in the Spirit. Second, Holy Spirit baptism is received subsequent to and distinct from conversion. Third, at the time the believer is baptized in the Spirit, he is *immersed* in the power of the Spirit. The door is opened for him to receive various gifts of the Spirit that empower him for his mission.[6] (Modern charismatics teach Spirit baptism in much the same way as the Pentecostals have taught it. Yet there are different emphases and ways of understanding Spirit baptism.)

Anthony Hoekema, who is not charismatic, underscores the fact that baptism in the Holy Spirit is the central doctrine of the charismatic movement. He writes:

> So basic is this teaching to the neo-Pentecostal movement that if you take this doctrine away from it, what you have left is no longer neo-Pentecostalism. The baptism in the Holy Spirit is an experience *distinct from and usually subsequent to conversion* in which a person receives the *totality* of the Spirit into his life and is thereby *fully* empowered for witness and service.[7]

Hoekema describes the neo-Pentecostal teaching on Holy Spirit baptism like this:

> Though the Spirit regenerates a man and enables him to repent and believe in Christ at the time of conversion, the Spirit does not come into the believer's heart *as a Person* who fills his life completely and who now dispenses the full complement of his gifts until the time of the Spirit baptism. . . . which is an experience distinct from and usually subsequent to conversion.
>
> In neo-Pentecostal circles, therefore, *one is not considered to have available to him the full power of the Holy Spirit until he has experienced Spirit baptism;* hence all Christians are urged to seek such a Spirit baptism.[8]

There is not total agreement on all points of the teaching of Spirit baptism, either between Pentecostals and charismatics or between one charismatic group and another. One thing

they all have in common, though, is a theology that emphasizes the postconversion indwelling, or infilling, of the Christian by the Holy Spirit as a person, resulting in a climactic,
ecstatic, power-loosening, love-forging, peace-instilling, joy-
provoking, evangelistic-empowering experience.

From the viewpoint of either the Pentecostal or the neo-
Pentecostal, if a Christian is without the experience of baptism
in the Holy Spirit, he is lacking a great deal of the power of the
Holy Spirit that could otherwise be available to him. Through
the experience of Holy Spirit baptism—not outside of it—this
full, personal indwelling of the Holy Spirit takes place, empowering the Christian for service in the world. This empowering
may even take the form of doing miracles in order to attract
unbelievers to the gospel. Therefore, every Christian should
seek the experience of Spirit baptism. Hoekema asserts:

> Central to neo-Pentecostalism is the teaching that every
> believer must seek a post-conversion baptism in the Spirit in
> order to obtain full power for Christian service and to receive
> the full complement of the Spirit's gifts.[9] In neo-Pentecostal
> literature the expression "baptism in the Spirit" is used to
> describe an experience *which every believer ought to have.*[10]

Larry Christenson, a Lutheran charismatic and therefore
one who describes Spirit baptism in relation to Lutheran baptism, points out that the charismatic movement, like the Pentecostal movement, emphasizes the Holy Spirit's infilling:

> This accent on the person of the Holy Spirit is linked to the
> experience of receiving or being filled with His presence.
> Precisely because He is a person, He must be received. . . . It
> is possible to hold the doctrine of the Holy Spirit, yet not
> experience His presence and power. *The doctrine must find
> expression in personal experience.* This is a fundamental per-
> ception of the charismatic renewal.[11]

Christenson stresses that all Christians have the Holy
Spirit but that Holy Spirit baptism involves the Christian in a
deeper way with the Holy Spirit:

> *Beyond conversion, beyond the assurance of salvation,
> beyond having the Holy Spirit,* there is a *baptism* with the

> Holy Spirit. . . . Sometimes the baptism with the Holy Spirit occurs spontaneously, sometimes through prayer and the laying on of hands. Sometimes it occurs after water baptism, sometimes before. Sometimes it occurs virtually simultaneously with conversion, sometimes after an interval of time. So there is considerable variety within the pattern.[12]

Christenson points out that the charismatics do not divide Christians into those who "only have salvation" and those who have the Spirit, as the classical Pentecostals tend to do. Rather, according to the charismatics, all Christians have the Spirit. No formal "second state" in the Christian life is taught, though there will be distinct experiences. Thus Christenson emphasizes that the two-stage theological model (conversion *plus* baptism of the Spirit, common to the Pentecostals) is being replaced with a more *organic* view, which understands that the Holy Spirit has been given as a gift to all Christians.

While in classical Pentecostalism the receiving of the Holy Spirit with a manifestation of his gifts (tongues, healings, prophecy, and so on) is supposed to occur later, apart from water baptism, charismatic tradition recognizes that the Holy Spirit is being given, together with his gifts, at the same time water baptism is applied. But whether these gifts are actually exploited as a result of baptism is another question. Christenson writes:

> In baptism one is given all the things (e.g., gifts, ministries, workings, services, etc.) that he will ever receive in Christ— potentially. But if that baptism is not actualized in the life of the baptized, God's purpose in baptism has failed of achievement. It *would have been better if the person had not been baptized at all.*[13]

Christenson gives us further insight into the teaching of Lutheran charismatics:

> One way in which this relationship [established between the Christian and God at the time of water baptism] may be expressed is *through a signal breakthrough or release of the power of the Holy Spirit.* . . . At this point we see a distinction between the Lutheran and the classical Pentecostal way of describing the bestowal and manifestation of the Holy

> Spirit. *The Lutheran sees it as a releasing of the Spirit which
> has already been given, for power and ministry. . . .* Classical
> Pentecostalism sees it as *an added endowment of
> the Spirit.*[14]

On the one hand, Christenson teaches that *every* Christian
has been "baptized with the Spirit" (in water baptism). But on
the other hand, he teaches that every Christian has not experienced "the event or process by which the power of the Holy
Spirit is released in a fresh way."[15]

Father Bennett of the Episcopal church defines Holy Spirit
baptism not as *getting* the Holy Spirit but *receiving* him, or
making him welcome. As a result, the Holy Spirit is permitted
to fill more areas of the Christian's life and to flow through
the Christian to the world.[16] Bennett also describes the baptism in the Spirit as a freeing of the riches stored in a Christian so that those riches can "break forth into the world."[17]

Jean Stone, the founder of *Trinity,* a charismatic magazine,
and a follower of Bennett, describes neo-Pentecostals as being
less emotional, and prone to speak in tongues at will after
they have received them. Furthermore, she states that
tongues are given a more private than public use in the neo-
Pentecostal movement. Stone also claims that in the charismatic renewal, the people involved are more Bible centered
rather than experience oriented, conducting more orderly
meetings with less emphasis on tongues.[18] This last statement
is not necessarily factual today. The emphasis on prophecy,
which is highly experience oriented, among some charismatics
has merited a warning from Pentecostals not to make the
same mistake they made when they gave prophecy too high a
priority. Stone's observation concerning a diminished emphasis on tongues is particularly true in a Catholic charismatic
setting.

Benefits claimed through Holy Spirit baptism

Both classical Pentecostals and neo-Pentecostals hold that
Spirit baptism makes all the gifts of the Holy Spirit—including
the supernatural ones—available to the church today. They
believe that God intends these gifts to be part of the church's

witness in all ages. The Pentecostal movement and the charismatic renewal have supposedly rediscovered Holy Spirit baptism and restored it to the church after long disuse, making it possible once again for Christians to receive the fullness of the Spirit and the use of his gifts.

Many individuals claim to have received a variety of blessings as a result of Spirit baptism and speaking in tongues. J. Rodman Williams, in *Christianity Today*, described the charismatic experience for Christians:

> God, who may have seemed little more than a token figure before, has now become vividly real and personal to them. *Jesus Christ, largely a figure of the past before,* has now become the living Lord. The *Holy Spirit, who previously had meant almost nothing to them,* has become an immanent, pervasive presence. . . . *Prayer, formerly little more than a matter of ritual,* and often practiced hardly at all, becomes a joyful activity often carried on for many hours. . . . The *Eucharist* has taken on fresh meaning under the deepened sense of the Lord's presence—the doctrine of the Real Presence has become experiential fact. . . . This "baptism with the Spirit" is wholly related in the charismatic movement to faith in Jesus Christ. It is ordinarily thought of not as a "second work of grace" but as a *deepening of the faith that is grounded in Christ* and the new life in his name.[19]

Strangely enough, this Spirit baptism seems to strengthen the ties holding many people to their churches. Charismatics in the ritualistic Episcopal and Roman Catholic churches claim to find deeper meaning in the prayers of the Mass and a greater enjoyment of the liturgy. After their Spirit baptism, many Catholics tend to go back to a fuller use of their traditions, such as praying the rosary and Mariolatry. Some avail themselves more frequently of the sacrament of penance and of daily attendance at the Mass and Communion.

While involvement in the charismatic movement has often led to divisions in the Protestant churches, with people leaving their churches to join others or to found new groups (especially at first), Catholics involved in the movement have not been affected in this way.[20] Rather, their love for "the great Catholic traditions" increases.[21] The charismatic movement within Roman Catholicism has injected "new life" without altering the "essential structures of the Church."[22]

Spirit baptism of non-Christians?

One idea that crops up every now and then in charismatic literature is that a non-Christian can also be filled with the Holy Spirit and that conversion either accompanies the Spirit's infilling directly or results from it. *In effect, Spirit baptism takes the place of the Sacrament of Baptism and the preaching of the gospel as the means of grace.* Stephen Clark speaks of the possibility of fallen-away Christians also receiving Holy Spirit baptism and of being born anew and joined to Christ through the experience.[23] He further mentions the possibility of a person's being baptized in the Spirit though only *partially* converted to Christ. Yet he adds the opinion that without full conversion the person will not be much of a Christian.[24]

Strangely enough, avowed non-Christians have claimed the baptism in the Holy Spirit and such gifts as speaking in tongues but without changing beliefs that make saving faith impossible. Thus they profess to be Spirit-filled but lack saving faith—an impossible situation. Robert D. Brinsmead writes:

> When the neo-Pentecostal movement was getting under way in the Los Angeles area in the early 1960s, I talked to an Assembly of God preacher about the phenomenon. He said, "we used to be leaders in experiencing the baptism in the Holy Spirit, but not since the Spirit has visited the great historic and Protestant Churches. I know an Episcopalian priest in this city who is so liberal he neither believes in the virgin birth nor the resurrection. Yet he has recently received the baptism in the Spirit and exhibits a marvelous power in his ministry." The Pentecostal preacher shrugged his shoulders and added, "I can't understand why God would give all that power to a fellow so far out on the liberal left." A few months ago a group of Pentecostal Christadelphians invited me to talk to them. Christadelphians not only deny the divinity of Jesus Christ, but also his preexistence before his birth in Bethlehem. They also deny the personality of the Holy Spirit. Yet here were a group of

Christadelphians who claimed the baptism in the Holy Spirit and spoke with tongues.[25]

Such happenings serve as a warning flag that we must carefully assess the foundation of this movement.

5

SPEAKING IN TONGUES AND INTERPRETATION

Pentecostals and charismatics believe that Baptism in the Spirit must be accompanied by certain spiritual gifts. In the next chapters we will look at some of the "gifts" that are most important to them. In this chapter we will examine the role speaking in tongues plays in the Pentecostal/charismatic movement.

The role of tongues-speaking

Pentecostals want assurance that they have been filled with the Holy Spirit. They look to the original Pentecost account when the disciples spoke in tongues after they had been filled with the Holy Spirit (Acts 2), and they desire that gift for themselves. They believe that speaking in tongues is necessary if they are to be sure that the Holy Spirit is now active in their lives. To them speaking in tongues makes the experience of Holy Spirit baptism something that can be both seen by others and placed at an exact time.[1] The Pentecostal church taught that in the absence of speaking in tongues, no proof existed that a person had received baptism in the Holy Spirit. It is *the* evidence. While it is true that some Pentecostals have retreated from this older and more absolute position, nevertheless, speaking in tongues as the necessary sign is still the general rule.

Classical Pentecostals (at least in North America) very zealously guard their distinctive doctrine of initial evidence, while many charismatics would not take such a strong position. To counter the claims of charismatics that they were filled with the Holy Spirit but did not speak in tongues, the Assemblies of God reinforced its stand on initial evidence by stating that no one receives the baptism in the Holy Spirit unless and until he speaks in tongues.

The teaching that tongues-speaking is the initial evidence is well illustrated in the following full-page ad that appeared some years ago in *The Victoria Advocate,* a newspaper in Victoria, Texas:

> Have you received the Holy Ghost? What are the steps to *Holy Ghost Salvation?*
>
> 1) Repent of your sins—Your part.
> 2) Be baptized in the name of Jesus Christ for the remission, or pardon, of your sins—Preacher's part.
> 3) Receive the Holy Ghost, with the initial evidence of speaking with other tongues—God's part.
>
> Do all speak with other tongues when they receive the Holy Ghost?
>
> Yes!

Because tongues-speaking is a supernatural way of praying, it is often considered as opening the way to interpretation of tongues, prophecy, and the other supernatural gifts of the Spirit. Donald Basham goes so far as to conclude that all nine gifts (including the gift of healing) listed by Paul in

1 Corinthians 12 are available "potentially" to any believer who has been baptized in the Holy Spirit and "theoretically" may be manifested by him.[2]

What about the person who has never undergone the Holy Spirit baptism and, therefore, does not speak in tongues? Are the Spirit's gifts available to him or not? Pentecostals would answer by saying, "Not ordinarily." Basham admits to having known instances that were both exceptional and rare when Christians unbaptized in the Spirit appeared to possess gifts that normally are associated with Spirit-baptized believers. According to him, the general rule seems to be that the nine gifts of the Spirit listed in 1 Corinthians 12 are reserved for those who are baptized in the Spirit.[3] However, Basham states that six out of seven Christians who have been baptized in the Spirit have never manifested any gift besides what he calls "their devotional tongue."[4]

Pentecostals distinguish between speaking in tongues as initial evidence of Spirit baptism and speaking in tongues as a gift of the Spirit. While everyone speaks in tongues initially as a sign of baptism with the Spirit (Acts 2), not everyone is later given the gift of continuing tongues (1 Corinthians 12–14) for daily Christian living. "Continuing" tongues-speaking has a twofold use: It can be used in a church service or prayer meeting, where it must be accompanied by inter-pretation (1 Corinthians 14:27), or it can be used on a per-sonal basis in the form of prayer that does not come from the intellect but is a way of praising God that is so deep in mean-ing it can't be expressed in words.[5] One sampling of pastors in the Assemblies of God church revealed that 69 percent employed tongues-speaking daily but that it occurred less fre-quently among the Pentecostal rank and file. In fact, polls show that only a small percent claim to speak in tongues (as a continuing gift).[6]

The late Donald Gee of the Executive Presbytery of the Assemblies of God in England and Ireland maintained that speaking in tongues is an act of speaking not to other people but to God (1 Corinthians 14:2). Gee regarded tongues not only as an initial sign but as the sign of an ongoing communi-cation with God in the Holy Spirit's power.[7]

People respond in different ways to the experience of speaking in tongues. Some report being filled with joy, drunk with ecstasy. Others relate a feeling of weightlessness and of soaring in the air. Some feel a warmth creep up their bodies. Others experience an electric shock. Some feel an uncontrollable urge to laugh, while others sob quietly. Some, though they have spoken in tongues, feel no different than they had before and tend to regard the whole matter as no big thing.

A person may feel inhibited by speaking in tongues at first, but eventually becomes impressed by it and wants to continue. Some have an intense feeling of well-being, a "spiritual high." Others feel at peace. Still others conclude for the first time in their lives that God really loves them. Morton Kelsey, who has been in contact with a large number of tongues-speakers, reports that all who have written of their first experience call it one of the most valuable and transforming experiences of their lives. They had been searching for something. In their tongues experience, they thought they had found it. Their lives were changed. They found it easier to love. Bible reading became easier, more fascinating, and more meaningful. Witnessing came naturally. Many claimed to be healed of illness at the time of the tongues experience or soon after it. It became possible for them to interpret their lives in a religious way. The spiritual realm became more real. Prayer became more frequent, the ritual of the church service more meaningful. Many became more generous in their church contributions, even finding it easy to tithe. Some found it easier to control their tempers and discovered a new joy in life. Others found in tongues-speaking a more profound way of expressing praise to God.[8]

It is noteworthy that Gerlach and Hine in their psychological study of Pentecostalism draw the conclusion that there would probably not be a Pentecostal/charismatic movement without the emphasis on tongues-speaking.[9] Where it has been dropped, the fervency and power of the Pentecostal revival is greatly diminished.[10]

Speaking in tongues as practiced among Pentecostals and charismatics

Much has been written about the nature of tongues-speaking as it is practiced among today's Pentecostals and charismatics.

By drawing on a wide variety of charismatic and noncharismatic sources, we will attempt to give the reader a picture of the nature and use of speaking in tongues and of what authors are saying about it. Before we continue, the reader should note that the author does not deny that God can bestow the ancient gift of speaking in foreign languages if and when the situation demands. As an example of this, we may consider the account of how in 1922 Reverend H. B. Garlock, a missionary deep in Africa, delivered himself and another man from certain death. While they were held captive in a village of cannibals called the Pahns, the missionary suddenly began to shake violently and to speak to the natives in their own language. The savages freed them, and in time they were converted to Christianity and became a peaceful people.[11]

It seems to be well established that people have been known to speak unlearned foreign languages in Pentecostal and charismatic meetings. In *They Speak with Other Tongues*, John Sherrill reports that a Jewish man was converted at the Azusa Street mission in Los Angeles when he heard a young lady address him in Hebrew. L. Grant McClung, Jr. maintains that believers at the Azusa Street mission prayer meetings often spoke in intelligible foreign languages:

> Many foreign immigrants were present in Los Angeles, and a number were attracted to the prayer meetings. In numerous cases they were converted through the powerful and convicting messages conveyed supernaturally to them in their own languages. Azusa Street recipients assumed that God was giving them the ability to preach in other lands and often discerned a call to a particular country based upon the language they had spoken.[12]

However, it needs to be pointed out that many Pentecostals who entered foreign mission fields thinking they had received the gift of foreign languages were disappointed to learn that they hadn't.

In another purported incident, a Jewish rabbi heard a man pray over him in flawless, beautiful Hebrew in a Pentecostal meeting.[13]

There are similar reports among the charismatics. The late Father Bennett claimed to have spoken in Nepali while blessing a group in Calgary, Canada. Though he had never heard the language before, a woman in the front row recognized his words as identical to those on a tape recording she received from her brother, a Jesuit missionary in Nepal.[14] Bennett also tells of a girl who began to speak perfect French when she was baptized in the Holy Spirit, as was determined by a French teacher standing nearby.[15] Sherrill tells of Harald Bredesen, who spoke in Polish and didn't realize it until a Polish man responded to him in that language and then asked him how he could speak Polish but not understand it.[16] Donald Basham reports that Ernie Gruen, an American Baptist preacher, spoke in the Japanese language not once but several times.[17]

In spite of examples that could be given of Pentecostals and charismatics speaking unlearned foreign languages, we should not get the impression that such a thing is commonplace. E. Glenn Hinson, for example, maintains that the foreign language spoken by Pentecostals and neo-Pentecostals seldom consists of more than occasional words or brief phrases of a foreign language mixed together with ecstatic speech. Thus he concludes that no ability to speak a foreign language was really given to the person.[18]

Some Pentecostals argue that the language of tongues is a true language or perhaps an archaic form of a language no longer spoken or even the language of heaven spoken by angels.[19]

According to some Pentecostals, the nature of tongues may be ecstatic speech, but it may be a language as well.[20] An article by Frank Farrell in *Christianity Today* titled "Outburst of Tongues: The New Penetration" contained the following statement meant to show that just because a Pentecostal's tongue cannot be identified, it does not mean it does not exist somewhere on the planet: "A Christian expert states that it is usually impossible to identify a given utterance as a language inasmuch as there are 3,000 languages, many of them unknown."[21]

The testimonies of linguists indicate that this theory is unacceptable. William E. Welmers, professor of African languages at the University of California at Los Angeles, wrote a letter to the editor of *Christianity Today* in which he takes exception to the above statement. His remarks are enlightening:

> The fact that there are some 3,000 languages in the world, many of them unknown (to most of us, that is), is not entirely relevant. We do know something about representative languages of every known language family in the world. I am by no means unique among descriptive linguists in having had direct, personal contact with well over a hundred languages representing a majority of the world's language families, and in having studied descriptions of languages of virtually every reported type. If a glossolalic were speaking in any of the thousand languages of Africa, there is a 90 per cent chance that I would know it in a minute. Now, I have also had the opportunity of making a sympathetic study of an alleged instance of speaking in tongues. And I must report without reservation that my sample does *not* sound like a language structurally. There can be [in the sample he heard] no more than two contrasting vowel sounds, and a most peculiarly restricted set of consonant sounds; these combine into a very few syllable clusters which recur many times in various orders. The consonants and vowels do not all sound like English (the glossolalic's native language), but the intonation patterns are so completely American English that the total effect is a bit ludicrous. My sample includes an "interpretation." At the most generous estimate, the glossolalic utterance includes ten or eleven "sentences" or stretches of possibly meaningful speech. But the "interpretation" involves no less than fourteen distinct and independent ideas. There simply can be no match between the "tongue" and the "interpretation." I am told that Dr. E. A. Nida of the American Bible Society has reported similar impressions of glossolalic recordings. Our evidence is still admittedly limited, but from the viewpoint of a Christian linguist the modern phenomenon of glossolalia would appear to be a linguistic fraud and monstrosity, given even the most generous interpretation of First Corinthians 12–14. . . . So far, I can only conclude, with all the sympathetic Scripture-centered scholarship I know how to apply, that modern glossolalia is a sad deception.[22]

Dr. Eugene Nida, the famed linguist mentioned in the above letter, draws the conclusion that a recording of glossolalia he examined "bore no resemblance" to any language that has ever been treated by linguists. Dr. Nida points out that the tendency is for the glossolalic to employ his own inventory of sounds and to produce from them sounds that have simulated "foreign features in nonsense combinations."[23]

Hamilton maintains that once the tongues-speaker has been able to regress and let go of the conscious controls, thus producing glossolalia, it becomes easy to repeat the same or similar sounds under a wide variety of conditions, not only when kneeling in church but also when driving on the freeway.[24]

Sherrill taped sessions of tongues-speaking that he later played to a group of six linguists. Not one of them recognized a known language from the tapes. Yet they did identify language patterns. Sherrill had secretly included two deliberately forged tongues-speaking sessions, one by his son and the other by his wife. Though the two had tried to imitate as closely as possible the sound of actual tongues-speaking, the linguists immediately recognized the deceptions and branded them as "just noise."[25] The difference in the speech patterns between the "natural" and the "forged" tongues-speaking is at least partially explained by the fact that the unconscious plays an important part in modern tongues-speaking, while the forgers were employing their conscious intellectual powers. The speaking performed in glossolalia "is not framed by the speaker in the way of a learned language. It is spontaneous linguistic expression; the speaker does not consciously determine what he or she is going to say. It does not proceed from the conscious reasoning process."[26]

William Samarin, another language expert, refers to glossolalia as "pseudo-language," a phenomenon rather than a language.[27] Samarin concludes that glossolalia, though it resembles a language, is not one. It contains neither grammar nor sentence division. The glossolalia syllables, which consist of consonants and vowels, find their main source in the native language of the speaker. Though glossolalia is not a language, Samarin would not call it gibberish either. He does not regard it as supernatural but as something normal. It is irregular but normal nonetheless. He does not even categorize it as extraordinary. Samarin states that anyone can produce glossolalia when he finds the trick to doing so. It lies in rediscovering the instructions one has had for learning to talk as a little child. This knowledge, which has been dormant in the person since childhood, comes to life when the person is given a reason to want to recall this knowledge and is shown how to become willing to do so.[28] Samarin feels that glossolalia becomes an abnormal phenomenon only when Christians believe it comes from God.

The mechanics of speaking in tongues

There are some documented examples of what speaking in tongues sounds like. A few months after Father Bennett was forced to resign as a pastor of Saint Mark's Episcopal Church in Van Nuys, California, *Time* magazine reported on a private prayer-meeting held by a few members of Saint Mark's who were followers of the charismatic priest. During the meeting a woman member began to speak in tongues. Her words were, "Da sheontee konomeki no sienti holay coriente no sheonte mees." She continued for about a minute in the same vein. Her own interpretation of her tongues-speaking was this: "The Lord thy God says unto thee that he is here in the midst of thee. . . . When you pray, fear not. He is with you always, and his love surrounds you like a fleecy cloud. Thus saith the Lord." Another member of Saint Mark's also spoke in tongues, saying, "Doyosi ki-i-yeno mayashi yekatona masi yano ma yenda ya kotano masiki."[29] In July 1960 *Newsweek* printed a message of one of Bennett's followers that went like this: "Kasina loma nisha ko siki da lotey misha da sika dita la den-tay." The alleged translation was, "I am the Lord thy God and I am with thee."[30]

Morton Kelsey, a charismatic, likens glossolalia to pig Latin or Chinese. He says that it is speech the speaker neither controls nor understands, made up of speech sounds that come haphazardly and spontaneously to the lips.[31] The person has no control over the words, which come automatically, but he often does control the speaking, being able to turn the experience on and off. Kelsey offers the following explanation of the mechanics of tongues-speaking:

Speaking in tongues is similar to the dream in all of these characteristics. In order to have the experience of glossolalia one must empty himself and give up conscious control, yielding himself to the experience. As in sleep the individual does not give up control to another person as he does in hypnosis or suggestion, but to something unknown which he seems to contact through the depth of himself. The experience of tongues is automatic, and one has no more conscious control of the words that come to his lips than the dreamer does of the images which come to him. . . . In tongues one portion of the conscious mind, as it were, goes to sleep and permits unconscious contents to flow through the physical apparatus which is normally subject to consciousness.[32]

Kelsey also calls tongues-speaking "a sleepwalking with one's vocal cords while still conscious."[33]

John P. Kildahl, a clinical psychologist, did research in glossolalia for the American Lutheran Church. Kildahl concludes that a person speaking in tongues gives up ordinary conscious controls over the production of speech.[34]

Larry Christenson refers to glossolalia as a spiritual exercise in which one prays or praises in tongues while his intellect is inactive.[35]

Donald S. Metz (one-time head of the department of religion at Bethany Nazarene College) states that modern tongues-speaking is for the most part not a product of the Holy Spirit's inspiration, nor is it demonically produced. Rather, he considers it to be a psychologically induced human reaction.[36] George B. Cutten claims that every case of tongues-speaking that has been "strictly and scientifically investigated" can be explained by "recognized psychological laws."[37]

Psychiatrist Stuart Bergsma, superintendent of Pine Rest Christian Hospital in Grand Rapids, Michigan, speaks of a number of experiences he has had with glossolalia: "All these [experiences] have left me with the conviction that glossolalia especially can be psychologically explained and is not, in general, a 'spiritual' phenomenon."[38]

Another Christian psychiatrist, Dr. Pattison, gives a similar view of tongues-speaking: "The product of our analysis is the demonstration of the very natural mechanisms which produce glossolalia. As a psychological phenomenon, glossolalia is easy to produce and readily understandable."[39]

The language expert Samarin suggests that anyone can produce glossolalia when he finds the "trick" in doing so and that glossolalia lies close to everyone.

Tongues-speakers find that after their first encounter with glossolalia, they can more or less turn it on and off at will and are even able to demonstrate the "gift" to others. Father Bennett, you may recall, did so on a Los Angeles television news broadcast.

While the mechanics of glossolalia can be explained psychologically, the issue of whether tongues-speaking in our day is or is not the gift of the Holy Spirit cannot be decided on the basis of psychological studies and psychiatric evaluations. The Word of God is the only norm by which the "spirits" must be tested. The United Presbyterian study of the charismatic renewal gives this timely warning: "It will be a dark and tragic day in the life of Christianity if psychological norms are to become the criteria by which the truth or the untruth of religious experience is to be judged."[40]

However, we do not wish to leave the reader with the impression that psychological and psychiatric evaluations of tongues-speaking are without merit. Quite to the contrary. These evaluations reveal that glossolalia in use by Pentecostals is for the most part not genuine language, but a form of spontaneous utterance, which can be produced in nonreligious context.

Moreover, tongues-speaking is not confined to Christians. Hindus, Muslims, and Mormons use it also. A good share of the Pentecostals and charismatics ask us to accept their premise that only those who have spoken in tongues are filled with the Holy Spirit. Yet what they accept both for themselves and for all of us as the initial evidence of the Holy Spirit's infilling is a phenomenon that can be induced psychologically in just about anyone. So the "unmistakable" sign of Spirit baptism emerges as quite mistakable, subject to human and demonic deception.

Getting the gift

How does one begin to speak in tongues? What gets the tongues-speaker going? Glossolalia can occur as two are praying together quietly or as a person is praying by himself. It can occur as a person awakens suddenly from sleep and finds himself speaking words he doesn't recognize or understand. Frequently, glossolalia occurs in a group of people, when one is praying for another to receive it and when others lay their hands on the seeker's head. It has been known to occur simultaneously with a group of people. Sometimes glossolalia occurs spontaneously to a person without his actually seeking the experience or even knowing what to make of it when it happens.

However, Pentecostals usually list certain conditions the candidate must meet to prepare for receiving the Spirit baptism: prayer, intense desire, and obedience. The latter includes both separation from sin, or active obedience, and yielding oneself completely to the Holy Spirit and to the experience. This is also called passive obedience.[41]

The "tarrying" meeting is very important to Pentecostalism. It is usually held after the regular church service (especially in the evening). At that time those who yearn to receive the Spirit baptism are both prayed with and prayed for. One object of the tarrying meeting is to help induce the initial evidence of Spirit baptism in one who has already experienced water baptism.

At such a meeting, the candidate may be told to let himself go and may begin speaking in tongues when hands are laid upon him. The Assemblies of God church lists seven instructions for helping a person receive baptism in the Holy Spirit. Among them, number 3 instructs him that when hands are laid on him, he is to receive the Holy Spirit, and number 6 instructs him to open his mouth. To help him along, the candidate may be encouraged to make certain elementary sounds such as "bah-bah-bah" to loosen the tongue and get him started. Other sounds may also be suggested. For example, sometimes the candidate is told to repeat the name of Jesus over and over.

Raymond J. Storms, a former Assemblies of God pastor, became turned off toward the whole tongues movement. He wrote a booklet about his experiences as a Pentecostal titled *I Chose Not to Be a Charismatic*. He had this to say about Pentecostal practices employed to get glossolalia started in candidates for Holy Spirit baptism:

> I was speaking with some Assembly of God ministers in a restaurant. The subject of Pentecostal shenanigans came up at the meal. One pastor told about a technique he had observed where the altar worker told the person seeking to be filled with the spirit to say "la la la" over and over rapidly. At first the candidate would be speaking in "heavenly baby talk," but soon he would learn to yield more fully to the Holy Spirit and he would speak a "mature tongue."
>
> Another technique used in bringing someone through to the "fullness of the Spirit" was to have the seeker breathe deeply over and over again until he had "breathed in the Holy Spirit." This technique might be responsible for a large number of folks being "slain in the Spirit."[42]

Storms concludes, "The Biblical pattern is a striking contrast to much of what I have observed in Pentecostal and charismatic circles."[43]

The neo-Pentecostal approach to tongues-speaking is not really different from the old Pentecostal approach. Those that have the "gift" help those who don't. They pray for and encourage the candidate. There is the laying on of hands and a keen expectation of what is about to happen. Sometimes words or sounds are furnished for the candidate to mouth, to trip his tongue. Larry Christenson is quoted as giving the following instructions to a candidate:

> In order to speak in tongues you have to quit praying in English. You simply lapse into silence and resolve to speak not a syllable of any language you have ever learned. Your thoughts are focused on Christ, and then you simply lift up your voice and speak out confidently, in the faith that the Lord will *take the sound you give Him, and shape it into a language.* You take no thought of what you are saying: as far as you are concerned, it is just a series of sounds. The first sounds will sound strange and unnatural to your ear,

and they may be halting and inarticulate. (Have you ever
heard a baby learning to talk?)[44]

John Sherrill, a reporter who set about to investigate Pentecostalism and the charismatic movement, himself became a
tongues-speaker. In reporting on how he began speaking in
tongues, Sherrill tells of feeling a tightening in his throat and
slowly losing his identity until finally his self-awareness disappeared.[45] In Sherrill's case, as he lost consciousness of self
he became aware of another "presence" in the room, which he
identified as Christ. He also heard a command that jolted him
away from coming back to reality, a command that told him to
look neither right nor left, but straight ahead.[46] Sherrill
described the tongues that finally burst forth from his lips as
not beautiful, but ugly. They were explosive, even grunting
sounds. Nevertheless, he was overcome with joy at hearing
them. For quite some time he continued to pray in his new
tongue, laughing as he did, and feeling that he was free.[47]

Sherrill's experience emphasizes what we have noted
before. In learning to speak in tongues, one forfeits conscious
control and places himself in the control of his subconscious.
The tongues-speaker believes, of course, that he is placing
himself under the control of the Holy Spirit. But where, we
ask, is the similarity between Sherrill's abandonment of self-
control and what happened in the book of Acts? The Holy
Spirit took the disciples by storm, before they had any chance
to "prepare" themselves.

The practice of tarrying, or waiting, for the baptism in the
Holy Spirit can certainly have tragic consequences for those
who do not receive the gift, especially when they are led to
think that speaking in tongues is the evidence that one is
saved. One charismatic told of praying for a woman who had
tarried for 14 years, all the while hoping she wouldn't die
because she had not yet been assured of salvation by speaking in tongues![48] The question asked by some Pentecostals—
"Are you saved?"—implies, "Have you spoken in tongues and
therefore proven your salvation?" I have had my own salvation called into question by overzealous Pentecostals simply
because I have never spoken in tongues or had the desire to
do so. Weak souls can be destroyed by this heresy or, at the

very least, be made to feel they are "second class" citizens in God's kingdom.

A perfect gift?

After the initial experience, does one retain his ability to speak in tongues? This seems to be the case especially among charismatics. One tongues-speaking clergyman from a major denomination states that the gift may remain with a person as years go by—usually in the same form that it first came to him.[49]

Pentecostals' and charismatics' permanent glossolalia is a "prayer-and-praise tongue." At prayer meetings this gift becomes a vehicle for prophecy, and the charismatic is regarded as God's spokesperson. Such speaking, according to J. Rodman Williams, is not meant to be an interpretation of Holy Scripture, but to go "beyond the words of Scripture."[50] The person who prophecies in tongues often lays claim to the gift of interpretation.

Some say the practice of speaking in tongues engenders a lasting confidence. But for others the very opposite is true. Consider the testimony of John Sherrill, whose tongues experience we mentioned earlier. About three months after his Spirit baptism, he experienced a violent reaction. He entertained suspicions that he was generating the whole thing himself, for he often mouthed nonsense syllables in an effort to start praying in tongues. Sometimes he was not successful.[51]

Pastor Larry Christenson admits that no gift of the Holy Spirit carries with it as many doubts, misgivings, questions, and misunderstandings as speaking in tongues.[52]

Richard W. DeHaan states:

> Many people who have come out of the Pentecostal movement are now convinced that they have been deceiving themselves. In a book written many years ago by Sir Robert Anderson we find the testimony of a Robert Baxter, a parliamentary lawyer in England, an Anglican and high churchman, who for a time felt a tremendous increase in spiritual power and seeming devotion to Christ due to the reception of the gift of tongues. Yet he later came to realize that that which for a time he had valued so highly was all a delusion.[53]

Raymond J. Storms, who had been a Pentecostal minister, writes: "I am convinced that many charismatics speak psychologically-induced tongues rather than Spirit-empowered tongues and some may even speak in tongues by the power of the devil."[54] This, from a former tongues-speaker.

There are others, of course, who attribute great benefits and blessings to tongues-speaking and who have remained with the tongues movement a long time.

The basis for Pentecostal/charismatic teaching

As one reads Pentecostal literature, it becomes clear that to a great extent, each writer draws his or her doctrine from personal observation and interpretation of events. While writers do point to passages of Scripture for some foundation for their teaching, experience itself becomes the greatest teacher. In fact, we can find some neo-Pentecostals who hedge on the question of scriptural proofs for Spirit baptism. Larry Christenson says:

> On the one hand, therefore, we recognize that the present-day experience is not foreign or contrary to Scripture. On the other hand, however, we realize that doctrine rests on clear apostolic teaching, not simply on the description of events. . . . Thus our consideration of the baptism with the Holy Spirit is meant to be *essentially descriptive of what is happening today, not normative of what is supposed to happen at all times and places.* . . . The question is *not,* "Is baptism with the Holy Spirit laid down as an absolute doctrine in the Bible?" The questions, rather, would be in this vein: "Is the *experience* that many people testify to *evidence of a genuine* visitation of the Holy Spirit? . . . Am I truly open to the full range of *what the Spirit wants to manifest in our church, or through me?*"[55]

In other words, in Pentecostal and charismatic minds, doctrine must also be formulated from human experience, not just from Scripture. Simply because they have an "experience," they assume it must be a genuine "Spirit-happening." They also consider it to be part of an ongoing manifestation of the Spirit and his gifts. Thus they insist that even though baptism in the Spirit cannot be proven precisely from Scripture, it is, nevertheless, something all Christians should accept and even seek for themselves *because it has been revealed for us in our time*. Christenson continues:

> For the most part, the charismatic renewal has avoided the pitfalls of the enthusiasts, the "super spirituals," who vexed Luther. . . . The enthusiasts were ready to set Scripture aside in favor of their own revelations. This finds no parallel in the charismatic renewal, where the Bible functions as the fountain, rule, and norm for faith and life. . . . Charismatics would agree wholeheartedly with Luther that the Spirit has tied himself to the external Word. . . . The Word describes the basic way in which we may expect the Holy Spirit to behave; the kind of objectives He has, the way He goes about achieving those objectives. *He will not act contrary to nor outside of that which He has caused to be revealed and proclaimed in the external Word*. . . . Charismatics understand the external Word in a *dynamic, not a static, sense. They do not see the once-for-all character of the gospel as ruling out the ongoing revelation of the Spirit*. Rather, it is the gospel itself which encourages us to expect ongoing revelation. Jesus did not say, "Lo, the Scriptures will be with you . . . Lo, my words will be with you . . ." He said: "Lo! *I* am with you always, to the close of the age" (Matt. 28:20). *The personal presence of the Lord, through the Holy Spirit, is the substance of our faith, and the ongoing expression of the gospel.*[56]

The gift of tongues-speaking in prayer and praise

Charismatics have added a new dimension and emphasis to speaking in tongues. Many today are claiming that this gift is a prayer-and-praise language that enables those who possess it to communicate directly with God for personal edification. Thus charismatics make personal benefit, not ministering to others, the main outcome of tongues-speaking.[57]

A writer in *Welcome, Holy Spirit: A Study of Charismatic Renewal in the Church* claims: "The gift of tongues is uniquely suited to private devotions, and this has been its primary application in the charismatic renewal. Many charismatics who have seldom if ever spoken publicly in tongues do so regularly in their private prayer times, and testify to its value."[58]

Just how highly this prayer-and-praise tongue is regarded among the charismatics is illustrated by the following testimony of a Lutheran charismatic pastor:

> I would not be in the ministry today if it had not been for the supernatural praise songs that came out of my inner being during a time of deep depression. The Holy-Spirit was sighing with words I didn't even want to sing. Praise God the victory over that depression came as Jesus Christ became the subject of my thoughts and words once again! Perhaps this is one of the reasons Satan has such a lying campaign against "speaking in tongues." This manifestation of the Spirit is basically another language to praise the Lord more abundantly.[59]

Father Bennett estimated, "Private speaking to God and praising God accounts for 99.99 percent of all speaking in tongues" among charismatics.[60]

In *The Charismatic Movement,* Bennett made the following observation concerning the so-called prayer-tongue supposedly given by the Spirit to charismatics:

> Speaking in tongues enables a person to speak or pray to God without interference from any human source, *including himself; without the mind or emotions or will intruding into the picture.* The indwelling Spirit says in effect, "I know what you need to express to God the Father. Trust me to guide you as you speak." Thus confession can be made of sins *that the mind does not even know about and would not acknowledge*, or would soften and rephrase if it did."[61]

The relation of speaking in tongues to Spirit baptism

In this chapter we have examined the Pentecostal/charismatic view of Spirit baptism and the gift of being able to speak in tongues. One final question will complete our picture of the place of tongues in the spiritual life of the Pentecostal and charismatic and help us get a better picture of the overall movement: Must a Christian who experienced Spirit baptism also speak in tongues?

Charismatics are divided into two groups. On the one extreme are those who consider tongues the indispensable sign of the Spirit's in-filling. On the other are those who do not emphasize the gift and say that speaking in tongues should neither be prayed for nor forbidden.

Representative of the first group is Father Bennett. To his way of thinking, a person may be *filled* with the Holy Spirit, but if he does not speak in tongues, he is not *baptized* in the Spirit. In his book *Nine o'Clock in the Morning*, Bennett recalled that his older son stuffed his fist into his mouth when he felt himself starting to speak in tongues because he was afraid he "wouldn't get it right."[62] Bennett concluded that his son had not received the Holy Spirit since he "wouldn't speak the language the Holy Spirit was providing."[63]

Bennett defined glossolalia as prayer in which the Christian, inspired by the Holy Spirit, prays directly to the Father, in Christ, without being limited by the intellect. He saw speaking in tongues as the person's yielding to the Holy Spirit for use as his instrument to praise God.[64] Unless one yields to the Spirit, one is not baptized in the Spirit. To Bennett the initial speaking in tongues is the beginning of the "prayer tongue" that will be used in private devotions.[65]

Howard M. Ervin, a neo-Pentecostal writer, is among those who would press the issue of speaking in tongues. He asserts, "Whether stated, or implied, it is a fair conclusion from the Biblical evidence, that tongues are the external and indubitable proof" of baptism with the Holy Spirit.[66]

Though speaking in tongues does not proceed from a person's intellect and though the meaning is obscure to the speaker, nevertheless, it is considered by charismatics to have great powers of edification. Ervin writes, "If the modern Christians went to church services having first 'edified' themselves in tongues, the average service would have more the tone of a jubilee than a requiem."[67]

Lutheran pastor Larry Christenson is representative of a more moderate approach to the necessity of tongues. He does not connect tongues-speaking to Holy Spirit baptism as *the* initial sign. Writing in *Trinity* magazine, Christenson states his belief that one cannot conclude from Scripture that those who have not spoken in tongues have not really received the Holy Spirit. To him, the book of Acts suggests a helpful pattern, that is, speaking in tongues is one way for a person to manifest the gift of the Holy Spirit.[68] Christenson's approach in his congregation is to pray not for the gift of tongues but for the Holy Spirit.[69] "Seek the Giver and not the gift" is a warning the more cautious charismatics take to heart.

One gets the impression that Christenson is struggling to claim neither too much nor too little for the experience. He asserts that the more hard-line doctrine of classic Pentecostalism has been "somewhat muted" by the charismatic movement, even though speaking in tongues is widespread in the charismatic movement.[70] Christenson points out:

> On the other hand, however, the distinctive experiential expectation of the Wesleyan-Holiness-Pentecostal tradition remains a *vital part* of the charismatic renewal. . . . And while there is no doctrine of speaking in tongues as the "initial evidence of baptism with the Holy Spirit," nevertheless the experience of tongues, as well as other spiritual gifts, is *expected and is in fact widespread.*"[71]

In his book *Speaking in Tongues*, Christenson writes: "To consummate one's experience of the baptism with the Holy Spirit by speaking in tongues gives it an *objectivity*. This objectivity has a definite value for one's continued walk in the Spirit, for speaking in tongues seems to have a definite bearing on the 'pruning' and 'refining' which a Christian must go through."[72]

Christenson's point is that tongues-speaking serves as an outward, objective proof of being baptized in the Spirit, displacing mere subjective claims. Although Christenson does not say tongues are indispensable, note the importance he places on them:

> The charismatic movement cannot be reduced simply to speaking in tongues. *Yet neither can it be understood or explained apart from* tongues. . . . Those who have experienced this manifestation of the Spirit find that it has great blessing and value. It is no "frill" or "extra" in their Christian life. . . . One speaks in tongues, for the most part, in his private devotions. *This is by far its most important use and value.* . . . The heightened awareness of God's pres-

ence is one of the greatest blessings one receives through this experience.[73]

Another charismatic has this to say about the important relation between baptism with the Holy Spirit and speaking in tongues:

> Speaking in tongues is the usual but not necessarily the only sign of experiencing the baptism in the Holy Spirit. One can be baptized in the Holy Spirit and not speak in tongues, but it is usually evident. The charismatic movement is a "tongues" movement, as is historic Pentecostalism, but "tongues" is not the essence of the movement. One can be baptized in the Holy Spirit and speak in tongues, yet still live quite worldly. Speaking in tongues does not mean that one has achieved a high level of sanctification or Christ-likeness. It does not mean that one is a mature Christian.

> The renewal probably would not exist without the baptism in the Holy Spirit and speaking in tongues, but the renewal is much more than these. Renewal is God's Spirit moving to draw people into a consciousness of God's presence, a putting away of the flesh, learning to live and walk by the Spirit and being able to enter into a consciousness of God. It's the human spirit released and joined with the empowering Holy Spirit, bringing a greater consciousness of the life possible through Jesus Christ. Renewal begins a life of sanctification in which one cooperates more with the Spirit of God.[74]

Catholics involved in the renewal are not unanimous on their answer to our question. Father Kilian McDonnell, a Catholic who has studied the charismatic movement in depth, reports that Catholic Pentecostals do not tend to be dogmatic on the matter of speaking in tongues as the necessary manifestation of the coming of the Spirit and the entry of his gifts. In fact, he says that they criticize the classical Pentecostals for this dogmaticism.[75]

Catholic writer Stephen Clark, like the Lutheran Christenson, wants to claim neither too much nor too little for tongues-speaking. He points out that a definite experience normally marks a baptism in the Spirit and that it is commonly the gift of tongues. Yet he criticizes the Pentecostals for going too far when they teach that without tongues-speaking one cannot receive Spirit baptism. Tongues-speaking is the *normal* first sign, not the *only* one. He concludes that if a person experiences the Holy Spirit living in him and working through him, then he is baptized in the Spirit.[76]

On the other hand, there are Catholic charismatics who go further in their testimonies. For example, Kevin and Dorothy Ranaghan write:

> From the day of Pentecost onward in Acts, speaking in tongues is a normal and usual result of the baptism in the Holy Spirit. . . . We are convinced that as far as the charismatic movement is concerned everyone touched by it is meant to pray in tongues, that in fact the gift of tongues is *always given by the Lord as he renews the life of the Holy Spirit.*[77]

The Ranaghans speak of the gift of tongues as "the externalization of the interior work of the Spirit" and call it "the threshold to a life of walking in the power of the Holy Spirit."[78] They also classify speaking in tongues as a manner of prayer that is meant to be a common and everyday experience for the Christian for the purpose of prayer and praise.[79]

On the other hand, another Catholic theologian, Dr. J. M. Ford, does not see the gift of tongues as normative for the Christian. She feels that those who claim that tongues-speaking is given universally to the church overstate the matter.[80] Ford is a professor of theology on the staff of Notre Dame University, which is close to the Catholic charismatic scene.

The interpretation of tongues

How Pentecostals and charismatics practice interpreting tongues is directly related to how they practice speaking in tongues.

Much of the interpretation of tongues in charismatic meetings is in the form of prophecy rather than translation. This is to be expected since most Pentecostal tongues are not known foreign languages. Not infrequently, the interpretation is much longer than the tongues-speaking it is meant to interpret. Donald Basham gives the example of a woman who spoke in tongues for no more than 15 seconds. The man who interpreted her words spoke for a full minute and a half. While her 15-second discourse consisted in a short phrase repeated several times, the interpretation did not include repetition. One of the explanations Basham provides is that what follows tongues-speaking may not be interpretation at all, but prophecy.[81]

Tongues and interpreting tongues are certainly subject to fraud. Otherwise sincere people may falsely feel that they are prompted by the Holy Spirit to interpret and then say whatever comes to mind, convinced it is a real interpretation. In regards to speaking in tongues and interpreting tongues, even the heretic Celsus admitted that "they give occasion to every fool or imposter to apply them to suit his own purpose."[82]

Dr. W. A. Criswell, pastor of the First Baptist Church in Dallas, Texas, tells of a seminary graduate who had majored in Hebrew attending a tongues meeting in California. He rose to his feet and quoted Psalm 1 in the Hebrew language and sat down. A man stood up, solemnly announced that God had given him the gift of interpretation, and proceeded to declare that this was a message dealing with women prophesying in the church.[83]

When we study what Paul says about interpreting a tongue, we will see that interpretation is just that, interpretation. It is not meant to give the interpreter a chance to prophecy his own thoughts.

6

HEALING, PROPHECY, AND
POWER EVANGELISM

In the last chapter we noted that Donald Basham believes that all nine gifts listed by Paul in 1 Corinthians 12, including the miracle gifts, are available "potentially" to any believer who has been baptized in the Holy Spirit.[1] Therefore, in theory all of them can be manifested by him.

The ability to perform healings can also be a sign that one has truly experienced baptism in the Holy Spirit. Healing has been made an important part of many Pentecostal/charismatic worship services and prayer meetings. Charismatic leader Larry Christenson asserts: "Healing was never meant to be an option in the Christian Church—something that's all right for those who like to go off on special tangents. The ministry of healing *is part of the gospel, and therefore it is an obligation.*"[2] Christenson goes so far as to claim that whether or not a church conducts a ministry of healing is a matter of obedience to the Lord.[3] Christenson is one of those who believe that gifts such as prophecy and healing can serve as initial signs of Spirit baptism in place of speaking in tongues. Still, he feels that these gifts are less common than speaking in tongues.[4]

The literature of Pentecostals and charismatics makes it clear just how important they consider the gift of healing to be. Next to articles on salvation in Christ and the baptism of the Spirit, stories of how people were healed fill their literature.

Father Kilian McDonnell, a Catholic who has studied the charismatic movement in depth, states that the gift of healing is found in all Pentecostal groups.[5] Healing finds a regular place on the agenda of Pentecostal services and prayer meetings, as well as charismatic meetings and conferences. Short arms and legs are said to have grown. Lumps have disappeared, and even goiters have been dispatched. *The Call*, Oral Robert's autobiography, is expectedly replete with such testimonies.

Pentecostals and charismatics advertise healing services. "Come one, come all, and be healed!" is the invitation and promise extended to the community. The healer tells the sick person: "God does not want you to be sick. God wants you well. God wills to heal you. Believe that God has the *power* to heal you and also believe that it is his will to do so." Sometimes the "Spirit-filled" healer lays hands on the sick person, and through this act he claims to transmit power to the individual who needs healing. Through the faith of the healer and the faith of the person who is sick, the healing takes place.

Today we have the phenomenon of healers who specialize in specific types of healing. One of the favorite "healings" employed by charismatics is the lengthening of short legs. This type of healing is often displayed at charismatic conferences and conventions. C. Peter Wagner points out in *How to Have a Healing Ministry without Making Your Congregation Sick:* "Speaking of gifts, do not be surprised to find that some with the gift of healing have been given specialties in certain areas. Francis MacNutt, for example, has had little success praying for deafness, but a fairly high degree of success praying for bone cancer. My specialty is for lengthening legs (which in most cases involves pelvic adjustments) and problems relating to the spine."[6] One can't resist asking the question: Where does this sort of thing fit in with the healings reported in the book of Acts or the healings performed by our Lord?

Forgiveness of sins ensures physical healing?

Those who stress faith healing tend to connect this gift to the gospel of Christ. "Christ," they say, "came to heal the *whole* person; Christ wants to forgive your sins, but he also wants to heal your body."

As the charismatic movement has matured, the teaching of healing the whole person has become deeply rooted and widely promoted. One author writes:

> Jesus heals a sick and fallen world. Poverty, famine and calamity are evidences of a sick and fallen creation. His feeding of the hungry and his stilling the storm are signs that he comes to heal the whole creation. . . . In essence, as we have seen, *physical healing is of one piece with such things as forgiveness or the final conquest of death. Therefore we should lay hands on the sick and pray for them to be healed with the same certainty that we proclaim the forgiveness of sin or preach the resurrection.*[7]

The author then draws a parallel from Jesus' healing of the paralytic man when Jesus announced: "Your sins are forgiven. I tell you, get up, take your mat and go home" (Mark 2:5,11). The writer concludes that physical and emotional healings are actually signs that tell a skeptical world that our gospel "is a gospel of total healing, *not just a stream of nice-sounding words.*"[8]

The charismatic renewal "declares that Christ's atoning work was as much for sickness as it was for sins, so the believer should accept Christ not only as sin-bearer but also as sickness-bearer."[9] Thus the claim is made that "evangelistic preaching should ideally be linked with a strong ministry of healing. That was how Jesus carried on his ministry and the disciples followed suit (Acts 4:29,30)."[10]

Faith healing and deception

After researching Pentecostal/charismatic literature for years, we have reached the conclusion that, while many exorbitant claims of healing are made, the proof *against* many, if not most, of these claims is overwhelming. Careful, even scientific, testing of purported healings has resulted in negative findings.

The late Kathryn Kuhlman is a case in point. Kuhlman conducted healing services in various cities, and these attracted people from far and wide. Dr. William A. Nolen (a medical practitioner and surgeon) set out to find proof that genuine miraculous healings had indeed occurred through her ministry. He was not trying to discover fraud; in fact, he hoped to discover that miracles had taken place. After thorough investigation, he reported his findings in a book titled *Healing: A Doctor in Search of a Miracle*. Among the conclusions he drew are these:

> A charismatic individual—a healer—can sometimes influence a patient and cure symptoms or a functional disease by suggestion, with or without a laying on of hands. Physicians can do the same thing. These cures are not miraculous; they result from corrections made by the patient in the function of his autonomic system.[11]

> Patients that go to a Kathryn Kuhlman service, paralyzed from the waist down as the result of injury to the spinal cord, never have been and never will be cured through the ministrations of Miss Kuhlman; Miss Kuhlman cannot cure a paralysis caused by a damaged spinal cord. The patient who suddenly discovers, at a Kuhlman service, that he can now move an arm or a leg that was previously paralyzed had that paralysis as a result of an emotional, not a physical, disturbance. Neurotics and hysterics will frequently be relieved of their symptoms by the suggestions and ministrations of charismatic healers. It is in treating patients of this sort that healers claim their most dramatic triumphs.

> There is nothing miraculous about these cures. Psychiatrists, internists, G.P.s, any M.D. who does psychiatric therapy, relieve thousands of such patients of their symptoms every year. Psychotherapy, in which suggestion plays

a significant role, is just one of the many tools with which physicians work.[12]

Dr. Nolen attended a Kuhlman service and, in fact, served as a volunteer usher. He concluded:

> Not once, in the hour and a half that Kathryn Kuhlman spent healing, did I see a patient with an obvious organic disease healed (i.e., a disease in which there is a structural alteration). At one point the young man with liver cancer staggered down the aisle in a vain attempt to claim a "cure." He was turned away, gently, by Maggie. When he collapsed into a chair I could see his bulging abdomen—as tumor-laden as it had been earlier. . . . Finally it was over. There were still long lines of people waiting to get onto the stage and claim their cures, but at five o'clock, with a hymn and final blessing, the show ended. Miss Kuhlman left the stage and the audience left the auditorium.[13]

Later, Dr. Nolen was given the opportunity to meet with more than 20 of the people who claimed cures. Dr. Nolen concluded that many who went up to claim their cures did so because they didn't want to embarrass Miss Kuhlman. Dr. Nolen concluded that the instant cures were all for ailments that no one can see, but ailments that are obvious took three days or more to cure—in other words, the cure, or the failure to cure, would come when an audience was not present to witness it. Miss Kuhlman did not want anyone to come up on the stage and claim a cure for an ailment that everyone could see was still there.[14]

Regarding his follow-up work with the Kathryn Kuhlman healings, Dr. Nolen states:

> I listened carefully to everything they told me and followed up every lead which might, even remotely, have led to a confirmation of a miracle. When I had done all this I was led to an inescapable conclusion: none of the patients who had returned to Minneapolis [to meet with Dr. Nolen] to reaffirm the cures they had claimed at the miracle service had, in fact, been miraculously cured of anything, by either Kathryn Kuhlman or the Holy Spirit.[15]

Kathryn Kuhlman serves as a good example of how faith healers operate. They are experts at employing personal charisma and charm, conducting highly emotional religious services, appealing to the deep desire on the part of the sick to be made well, and fostering the belief that the "healer" is a personal emissary of a gracious and powerful God to bring about healing to the afflicted.

All this is effective psychotherapy in action. Furthermore, faith healers promise to accomplish what the medical doctors failed to do—to heal. Dr. Nolen describes the mood that was created at the healing service he attended: "You wanted to believe so badly you could hardly stand it. You didn't want to reason; you wanted to accept. . . . The whole scene— the religious fervor . . . casts a spell over the audience . . . it becomes almost more difficult not to claim a cure than it does to claim one."[16]

Pastor Don Matzat, a Lutheran theologian and author who once was a leader in the charismatic renewal, has some harsh words for the "healings" claimed by the tongues-speakers:

> That yearly Lutheran conference [on the Holy Spirit in Minneapolis], which hopefully has been put to rest, was certainly not a demonstration that the conference leaders and speakers had been ushered into the dimension of the supernatural through the doorway of "the baptism in the Holy Spirit." Some years ago "miracle worker" John Wimber was one of our speakers. Early in the week he told the assembly that on Friday evening, the final night of the conference, we would have a healing, miracle service. It was my job to introduce him on that Friday evening. I did so with much nervous anxiety, believing that I was in the presence of a powerful "man of God." But, much to our dismay, *nothing ever happened*. Wimber told us about all the miracles he had performed in the past but never demonstrated anything.[17]

In another article, published in *Christian News,* Pastor Matzat has this to say:

> Because the theology of Pentecostalism and the charismatic movement defines "the baptism in the Holy Spirit" as an empowering experience which ushers the individual into the spiritual dimension in which the supernatural "gifts" of

the Holy Spirit are readily available, the manifestation of such supernatural "gifts" in the form of a demonstration is vital for the credibility of the movement. The performance of miracles, primarily in the area of physical healing, is very important in order to confirm the definition of what the "baptism in the Holy Spirit" is all about. Those who can perform or claim to perform healing miracles will gain much popularity.

It is not at all surprising that this "miracle pressure" leads to deceit, lying, exaggeration or embellishment of experiences in order to establish a popular and successful ministry. . . . The God of Scripture becomes the God of reality and moves in the midst of his people with the same power as in days of old. . . . I have become very skeptical of and cynical towards charismatic healing claims. I recently received a mailing and newspaper advertisement [concerning] the healing ministry of Charles and Francis Hunter. They would be staging one of their healing demonstrations in the New York area. Many healing testimonies were recorded in the newspaper. *I did not believe the claims!* As far as I was concerned, it is a fraud which will be revealed as such. The "Oral and Richard [Roberts] fiasco" regarding raising the dead is in my estimation an example of "daddy lying and sonny swearing to it." I am disgusted by the television antics of Robert Tilton who offers his prayer towels, claiming that they contain healing power because he allegedly touched them. . . . Healing is a sovereign work of God. God can choose to confirm the Gospel in any given age through signs and wonders. But, is God, according to charismatic claims, doing so on such a massive scale today? From what I have seen and experienced, he is not![18]

Charismatic J. Lee Grady, an editor and writer of charismatic literature, also has some harsh words for charismatic "healings":

Many charismatics have taken healing to an extreme. We have promoted the idea that God wants to heal all people instantly of all their infirmities—cancer, head colds or hangnails. This has created embarrassment, hurt and misunderstanding, since all people who seek healing are obviously not cured. It becomes more distressing when certain ministers who claim a special "healing anointing" use smoke and mirrors to give the impression that people are healed when they are not. . . . We must stop promoting the simplistic idea that God intends us to vanquish all sickness and death.[19]

Many of those who shout the loudest about their gift to heal use their "gift" for mercenary purposes. We need furnish no names. Anyone who has followed the issue in the press in recent years is well aware of scandals that have been exposed in this regard, scandals that have rocked the church and brought shame to the name of Christ.

In a later chapter we will take up the subject of faith healing again, thoroughly scrutinizing it in the light of Holy Scripture.

Charismatics and the gift of prophecy

Charismatics and Pentecostals emphasize the gift of prophecy in the *narrow* sense, claiming direct revelations from God. The prophet addresses these revelations to the individuals or to the church. "The Lord told me," "the Lord gave me a message for you," and "the Lord said" are commonly heard expressions among tongues-speaking groups.

Charismatic leader Larry Christenson writes: "The charismatic renewal has recalled the church to *more spontaneous modes of revelation,* a wholesome complement to the emphasis on purely rational processes and conclusions. . . . Prophecy, visions, and spontaneous revelations are elements of the Christian heritage which the charismatic renewal has sought to recover for the church."[20]

"Prophetic" messages of the garden-variety charismatics are usually brief and consist of general exhortations to individuals or groups, urging them to be faithful. Many also claim to be endowed with information regarding the future or information that is supposed to solve a vexing problem. However, sometimes it happens that "prophets" will have messages supposedly from God that place the "prophets" in disagreement with each other, resulting in arguments. Pentecostal/charismatic prophecies of future events often miss the target, something that true prophecies never do.

Frequently, prophesying carried on among charismatics and Pentecostals can best be described as "quirky mysticism."[21] Prophecy is a very personal thing, consisting of a message purported to have been received directly from an angel, a saint, or God himself. As such, it is a message to which no other person has access. Modern prophets claim to have access to "inside" information from heaven and therefore have the right to bind the consciences of believers to it.

In the charged atmosphere of a Pentecostal/charismatic meeting, when the supernatural is expected to occur, would-be prophets are given an open forum to promote their own private agendas and pass them off as messages from heaven. This results, often enough, in charismatic chaos and confusion, especially when potshots are taken at others or when false doctrines are promoted or when the message breathes legalism and does not edify.

Too often, "prophecy" degenerates into a person grabbing for the spotlight. Or it becomes a vehicle for venting anger and frustration. It can also be used by a lone person to intimidate an entire group or assembly to see things his way. Don Basham contends that the Pentecostal movement has largely retreated from personal prophecy because of the problems and abuses to which it led.[22] He admits that he has been at meetings where the prophetic messages were not only less than edifying but downright garbled and confused. He further admits that prophets can be egocentric, rash, and offensive.[23] They will often have "messages" from the Lord for other people but seldom for themselves—usually a monotonous and stereotyped exhortation to be faithful.

The "now word" of the Lord

Charismatic leadership especially employs prophecy to their great advantage in what is often termed the "now word" of the Lord. Pastor Don Matzat gives us some valuable insight regarding this element of charismatic, prophetic utterance:

> Within the Charismatic Movement, we confront a different style of leadership. The communication of the prophetic "now word" of the Lord spoken by self-appointed and self-perpetuating charismatic leadership is a very important ingredient for the direction of the renewal. Charismatics believe that they are in the "move of God" or in the main-

stream of divine activity in the present age. For this reason, charismatic leaders seek to discover the will and direction of God for the movement, and communicate that direction to the people as if they are the divine spokesmen and their message is the will of God. The primary purpose for the large national or regional charismatic conferences is to allow the leaders the opportunity to bring the "now word" of the Lord to the people.

These subjective "now word" proclamations brought by the charismatic leaders and self-proclaimed prophets within the movement produce much confusion and in fact lead many astray. The "now words" turn out to be mere human opinion which never accomplish the intended purpose for which they were spoken.

In some cases, people have made important decisions affecting their lives and livelihood on the basis of these "now words." I know of a congregation who began erecting a much larger structure in order to prepare for the fulfillment of a prophetic word and vision given to them. Sad to say, they ran out of funds and have been strapped with a massive debt. More often than not, these massive visions are better defined as wishful thinking on the part of the spiritual leaders rather than direction and intention on the part of God.

It is a very serious matter to claim to speak for God. Recognizing the majesty, the power and holiness of God, one is unable to calculate just how serious it really is. In the Old Testament, if a prophet claimed to be speaking for God and his prophetic word did not come true, the prophet was stoned to death. If a person claims to be speaking a "now word" of the Lord and that word does not come true, he simply cannot say, "Oops, I was wrong!" Great damage is done to the name of the Lord and to the people of God by those who claim to be speaking for God.

[These] prophets flippantly use the name of God, declaring their words as if they were God's words. Do they stop and think how jealous God is of his name before they declare, "Thus saith the Lord?"[24]

Religious leaders often end theological debate and win the point merely by injecting a "now word" of the Lord: "The Lord just gave me a revelation. He told me . . ." With continual revelations from God, any point can be proven, any expenditure by the group—and the offerings to cover it—can be mandated by the leader, and any adversary can be silenced. It can be used to extricate the leader from hopeless situations and to cover his embarrassing personal blunders. Employing the "now word" of the Lord, charismatic leaders can redirect the course of a prayer group, a church, and even the charismatic movement itself.

David Edwin Harrell, in *Oral Roberts: An American Life*, tells about Oral Roberts' propensity for "direct messages from God," which messages accounted for most of his alienation from the outside world.[25] Harrell quotes one critic who said, "After a while it doesn't take much imagination to figure out that Oral and God are rather synonymous." Harrell points out that "[Oral's] revelations were a problem for his friends, as well. . . . [They] imposed a tyranny, however benevolent, within his organization."[26] According to the recollection of Al Bush, one of his staff, "If you'd walk in [to his office], he'd say, 'Oh, God just told me.' . . . That was his favorite line."[27] Even his "best friends in Tulsa cowered" when he brought a revelation, supposedly from God.[28]

Dave Hunt in *Beyond Seduction: A Return to Biblical Christianity* makes the point that the false teaching concerning "revelation knowledge" that was once confined to fringe Pentecostal and charismatic groups is beginning to spread rapidly throughout the church. He explains that this knowledge can be understood in two ways:

> 1) that a proper understanding of Scripture does not come through *interpretation* but through *revelation* (given only to certain leaders), and 2) that these prophets also receive "ongoing prophetic revelation" that supplements the Bible and must be accepted by the church as the key to a "great move of God" that will establish His kingdom upon earth. . . . The new revelations, which the church allegedly needs in order to move on in maturity, come through a class of prophets who are *not to be judged. And since "judging is out of order," only these self-appointed prophets can decide who they are, for no one who is not on their level is competent to make that judgment.*[29]

The point that must be emphasized over and over is that
the Holy Spirit is a God of truth, not of falsehood. He loves
truth and hates every lie (Acts 5:1-11). Of course, it is impossible to analyze every prophecy spoken by every charismatic
leader. But when it can be shown that the prophecies of a
movement lend themselves to subjectivity and are often
proven to be false, Christians must beware those in the movement who claim the gift of prophecy.

Power evangelism—proclamation followed by demonstration

When the charismatic renewal first made its appearance,
the emphasis was on the personal experience of the Holy
Spirit through Holy Spirit baptism. This found expression in
speaking in tongues, prophecy, prayer, praise songs and other
special forms of worship, Bible study, and sharing Christ and
the charismatic experience with one another.

In the mid 1960s, as the charismatic renewal began to
mature, the focus shifted from the initiatory event of baptism
with the Holy Spirit toward "the value of charismatic experience for ministry, spiritual growth, and the formation of
Christian community." The initiatory experience is still
emphasized and remains an integral part of the renewal, "but
it has less overall prominence than it did when the movement
first broke on the scene."[30]

As time passed and the charismatic renewal matured even
more, a missionary zeal developed for reaching out to the
world with the gospel of Christ. This heightening of missionary zeal, with world evangelization as the goal, was clearly in
evidence by the mid 1980s.

Pentecostals and charismatics both consider their movements to be the powerful thrust by the Holy Spirit to evangelize the world. This goal is to be accomplished, they claim, by
employing what has been labeled "power evangelism." C.
Peter Wagner, professor of church growth at Fuller Theological Seminary in Pasadena, California, comments on what he
calls "power encounters" carried on by missionaries among
tribal groups. "A power encounter is a viable, practical demonstration that Jesus Christ is more powerful than the false

gods or spirits worshiped or feared by a people group."[31] In other words, through power encounters, the Christians who are evangelizing heathen groups can demonstrate: "My God is more powerful than your god. That's why you should believe in my God." One of the first to use the term "power encounters" in missionary theory was missiologist Alan Richard Tippett, who introduced the idea in his book *Verdict Theology in Missionary Theory* in 1969. It amounts to battling evil forces not just with the word of the gospel but also with miracles—displays of divine power.[32] The late John Wimber, founder of the Vineyard Fellowship, one of the leading proponents of power encounters, stated:

> By power evangelism I mean a presentation of the gospel that is rational but that also transcends the rational. The explanation of the gospel comes with a demonstration of God's power through signs and wonders. . . . Power evangelism is evangelism that is preceded and undergirded by supernatural demonstrations of God's presence.

> Through these supernatural encounters people experience the presence and power of God. Usually this takes the form of words of knowledge, . . . healings, prophecy, and deliverance from evil spirits. In power evangelism, resistance to the gospel is overcome by the demonstration of God's power in supernatural events, and receptivity to Christ's claims is usually very high.[33]

Pentecostals and charismatics can indeed point to extraordinary church growth where miracles such as healings are combined with the gospel message. In promoting his kind of missiology, Wimber pointed out that on a worldwide scale, an estimated 70 percent of all church growth is among Pentecostal and charismatic groups.[34] C. Peter Wagner of Fuller Theological Seminary concludes:

> What I'm seeing, as the picture is beginning to emerge, is that worldwide there is a remarkably close relationship between growth of the church today and the healing ministry—particularly, but not exclusively, in new areas, where the gospel has just penetrated, where the devil has had complete reign for centuries or millennia. When the gospel first penetrates a

region, if we don't go in with an understanding of and use of
the supernatural power of the Holy Spirit, we just don't make
much headway. In Brazil 40% of the population are practicing
spiritists and another 40% have had some direct experience
with it. The way the gospel is spreading there is by confronta-
tion: healings, miracles, signs, and wonders.[35]

Jim Roberson, an LCMS pastor, declares:

That power [to do miracles] is not an option in the church
today; it is a necessity. The baptism with the Holy Spirit,
tongues, evangelistic power, prophecy, visions and dreams
are not optional. They are necessities for the Kingdom of
God on earth today as God guides and directs the work he
has for his people, revealing his will and manifesting his
power by the Holy Spirit."[36]

Oral Roberts once remarked, "I personally do not believe
that the gospel can be *fully* preached without signs and
wonders."[37]

7

DISTURBING DEVELOPMENTS
IN THE CHARISMATIC MOVEMENT

In its early years, Pentecostalism was known for its excesses, which turned many people off to the movement and to a great extent kept it from catching on with middle-class America. However, over time, excesses that were obnoxious to many (for example, the ranting and raving, the wild outbursts of emotion, and much of the exclusiveness) have been eliminated or toned down, with the result that Pentecostalism has become a more respected religious expression.

But while Pentecostalism has been jettisoning much of its excess baggage that proved to be burdensome, debilitating, and isolating, the charismatic movement has been busy acquiring baggage of its own. Over the past three decades, extremism has surfaced, teachings have been adopted, and claims have been made that have proven injurious both to the movement itself and to the people in it. We will now turn our attention to some of the more outstanding developments in the charismatic movement that deeply disturb our Christian senses.

Fraud and deceit in some, gullibility in others

Leaders in every Christian denomination struggle with their sinful natures, and from time to time, it becomes clear that some have allowed the sinful nature to have its way. Such was the case in Paul's day, and it will remain so until the end. Members in all denominations suffer from the malady of accepting everything their leaders tell them without maintaining a constant program of Bible study so they can be sure that what they are being told agrees with Scripture. In every day and age, some leaders within the church offer more than they can deliver, and they find an ample supply of people who succumb to the sensational. Pentecostals and charismatics do not have a corner on problems within their movement.

However, the movement itself is fueled by what we consider to be doctrinal errors that cannot help but foster the type of developments the following writers describe.

James Lee Grady, an insider to the charismatic movement, urges everyone who identifies with the charismatic renewal to examine the quality of what the charismatics have been constructing over the past three decades. He warns against "false prophecies, fabricated anointings, exaggerated claims and empty boasting." He calls for grounding the movement in Christ, building the church according to Christ's Word, and fashioning it with integrity.[1]

We noted in Chapter 6 Grady's concern with charismatic healing. He bemoans the fact that while charismatics tend to boast that they proclaim the gospel of Christ not only in words but also in power, the sad truth is that some of the charismatics' power is little more than illusion.[2]

Pastor Don Matzat, at one time a Lutheran charismatic leader, points out the deception and fraud that led to his leaving the movement:

Beginning as early as 1979 I found myself becoming increasingly disenchanted with the whole charismatic arena. Deceptive teachings such as inner healing, slain in the Spirit, the prosperity/faith teaching, creative visualization were becoming very popular within the movement, causing me to become less and less desirous of maintaining the "charismatic" label.

I found it very disturbing that charismatic speakers set forth so many wide-eyed prophetic claims depicting the many great things that God is going to do in and among charismatics. The claims are depicted as the "now word of the Lord." But in reality, God never does any of it. It was very disillusioning. I arrived at the conclusion that if people are interested in discovering what God *was not* going to do they should listen carefully to what charismatics claimed He *was* going to do. As a result of gullible charismatics "buying into" such outlandish prophetic claims there must exist literally thousands of disillusioned, disenchanted, disappointed, deceived charismatics wandering within the Church.[3]

In another negative critique of the charismatic movement, Matzat claims that the healing deception begins with the so-called baptism in the Holy Spirit, which itself is an erroneous definition of the Spirit's work:

Any pastors going through the negative experiences of dryness in the pulpit or trials in the ministry should pray and meditate upon the Word of God "until the Holy Ghost comes." Such enlightening work of the Holy Spirit is a promised, on-going reality. Erroneously defining this enlightening work of the Holy Spirit as being "the baptism in the Holy Spirit," a singular experience which opens the doorway into the supernatural, is the cause of the many charismatic aberrations. Because of this definition, demonstrating the reality of that supernatural dimension must, of necessity, become a charismatic priority. This leads to deception, involvement with occultism and mysticism, and a wide variety of sham demonstrations. Many charismatic pastors are under pressure to perform, to do some supernatural tricks and thereby be a "good charismatic." Charismatic people, rather than growing in their understanding of the Word through the enlightening work of the Holy Spirit, become experience happy, chasing after and supporting miracle ministries which seemingly prove their erroneous definition. Yet, such miracles at close examination are at best suspect. Foolish charismatics continue to send their financial support to those "great men of God" who claim to heal the sick and raise the dead.

For years I was involved in the large Lutheran Conference on the Holy Spirit in Minneapolis. Many of these "great men of God" were some of the conference speakers. Yet, in all those years I never actually saw a "miracle" happen. The wheel chairs rolled in and the wheel chairs rolled out again.

I believe it is time that Lutheran charismatics set aside their loyalty to Pentecostal theology and redefine their experience. The charismatic definition of "the baptism in the Holy Spirit" is neither in line with Scripture nor in line with the reality of what is actually happening. Such a definition continues to promote the charismatic "miracle sham." While many leaders within the Lutheran charismatic movement will be "good charismatics" and defend the miraculous, yet many of them realize very well that such miraculous events are very few and far between (if present at all) in their own lives and ministries. Why promote the sham? It is time to redefine and bring some Word-based stability into the lives of those who believe that they "got the baptism in the Holy Spirit" and are now moving in the supernatural. Both Scripture and experience demonstrate that such is not the case![4]

While there is deception in the charismatic movement, there is also a high level of gullibility on the part of the people who consider themselves to be of that special class of Christians. Forever connecting the blessing of being Spirit-filled with the ability to do miracles, they are often willing to follow illusion and accept deception. They are so filled with the expectation of miracles (such as demonstrated in "healings" and "prophecy" and "speaking in tongues") that they see genuine miracles where there are none.

Again, we call on James Lee Grady for his expert testimony as an insider. He points out that charismatics have been duped by men and women who claim to possess special spiritual powers, because they fervently desire to witness the Holy

Spirit's power restored in the church. They may be open to the supernatural in a naive way, which then invites deception.[5]

Grady complains that charismatics are prone to deifying human beings. Charismatics want to make into a god the person who may occasionally experience the gift of miracles in his ministry. Grady especially singles out Paul Cain as an example. Cain is a well-known modern-day prophet, who is very popular on the charismatic circuit. But in spite of all the hype surrounding his prophecies, do they come true? Grady reports his personal observation that in a charismatic meeting in San Antonio, Texas, in 1989, Cain spoke prophecies that were mostly inaccurate. Grady warns that charismatics are treading on dangerous ground if they build their lives naively on the words of any man or woman who claims to speak for God. And he further observes that even if Paul Cain did receive information supernaturally from God during that meeting in San Antonio, something dangerous was operating in the convention hall that night. "Thousands of Christians had put Cain on a pedestal where no man or woman belongs. People expected him almost to be like God. It was a setup for disappointment."[6]

Trends in charismatic worship

In an article in *Christianity Today* titled "Piety on Fire," J. I. Packer outlines "a recognizably charismatic approach to Christian and church life." The following are distinctive elements of charismatic worship:

6. Insistence that worship is central in the church's common life, and that the heart and climax of true worship is united praise as distinct from preaching and Eucharist (which have been the historic focal centers of Protestant and Roman Catholic worship respectively.)

7. The cultivation of a relaxed, leisurely, intimate, informal style of corporate worship, aimed at evoking feelings of awe and joy before the Lord and at expressing love and loyalty to him for his saving grace.

8. The use for this purpose of simple, repetitive choruses and "renewal songs," often consisting of biblical texts set to music in a modern folk idiom for performance with guitar accompaniment. . . .

9. The congregational practice of "singing in the
Spirit"—that is, sustaining ad lib, and moving within,
the full-close chord with which a hymn or song ends,
vocalizing extemporaneously and sometimes glossolal-
ically in the process.

10. Encouragement of physical expression of the spirit of
praise and prayer by raising hands, swinging the body,
dancing, prostrating oneself, and other such gestures.
Bodily movements of this kind are held to deepen worship by intensifying the mood being expressed, and thus
to glorify God.

11. Expectation of prophecy in worship gatherings, either
as an immediate on-the-spot message from God or as
the remembered fruit of a vision or a dream, and the
provision of opportunity to utter it to the congregation.

12. The typical perception of people both outside and inside
the community of faith less as guilty sinners than as
moral, spiritual, and emotional cripples, scarred,
soured, and desperately needing deliverance from
bondage in their inner lives; and the structuring of
counseling and prayer ministries to meet their need,
thus viewed.

13. The practice of prayer with laying on of hands, for all
who desire it, as a regular conclusion to worship gatherings. Those who are sick, disabled, and troubled in mind
are particularly urged to receive this ministry, and to
expect benefit through it.[7]

Packer also writes:

In recent years a growing number of charismatic and mainline denominational churches are integrating dance into
their worship. The liberal churches call it "liturgical dance,"
the charismatics call it "praise dancing." With charismatics,
ecstatic "dancing in the Spirit" is recently giving way to
widespread acceptance of spontaneous and choreographed
"dancing before the Lord."[8]

In considering the charismatic type of worship today, one of
the authors of *Pentecostals from the Inside Out* concludes: "I'm
grateful for what the charismatic movement has brought with
regard to celebration. But it seems steeped in a very humanis-

tic, materialistic kind of orientation. We need more than celebration. We need that balance of the Word and Spirit. We
need to anchor it solidly in the Word of God."[9]

We agree with David W. Cloud, who says that one reason
for Pentecostalism's popularity is that its worship services are
entertaining. He writes:

> Not content with [the jazzed-up music and wild antics of
> traditional Pentecostalism] the modern charismatic move-
> ment has gone "whole hog" into every sort of entertainment:
> rock music, drama, the dance, clowns, rap music, you name
> it. Charismatic television broadcasters pioneered the slick
> Hollywood-type Christian performances so common now in
> large charismatic churches. *Charisma* magazine is a show-
> case for this type of thing. The ads just ooze with worldly
> types of entertainment. And entertainment is always at the
> very heart of charismatic meetings such as New Orleans '87
> and Indianapolis '90.[10]

Charismatic worship really forms a contradiction. It emphasizes praise, but de-emphasizes the importance of doctrine. But
praise to God ought to be based first of all on doctrine, for doctrine reveals God as he truly is and how he works in the lives
of his people. Much of the praise singing of the charismatic
renewal is a seemingly endless repetition of a simple line, and
it expresses very little of God's truth and glory. The spontane-
ity of many charismatic worship services, in which on-the-spot
prayer, speaking in tongues, prophecy, and testimony (to say
nothing about holy laughter and falling down under the Spirit)
tends to generate the very chaos and confusion that Paul
attempts to dispel with this rule: "Everything should be done
in a fitting and orderly way" (1 Corinthians 14:40).

James Lee Grady writes:

> Let's ask ourselves: Can unbelievers who visit our Sunday
> morning services encounter the living Jesus? Or is the Jesus
> we preach some bizarre aberration, a Jesus whose primary
> interest is in giving us goose bumps or luxury cars? Can
> unbelievers who visit our churches find the Holy Spirit? Or
> do they find nothing more than a charismatic show, full of
> theatrics but devoid of spiritual substance? Do they find the
> Gospel or a nuts-and-bolts exhortation on how to grow a con-

gregation to a mega-church level? We charismatics tend to think that as long as our church services are "exciting," meaning full of loud praise music and motivational sermons, sinners will find Jesus when they happen to wander in. . . . In all our emphasis on the Holy Spirit's ministry and gifts and power, let's be careful to magnify the One the Spirit came to magnify.[11]

Slain in the Spirit

Charismatics desire a special anointing by the Holy Spirit through an experience—something they can feel, something physically and emotionally evident, something climactic. In some charismatic churches, one of the most popular of such experiences—if not the standard—is the condition of being "slain in the Spirit." After being prayed over, the person "slain in the Spirit" slumps onto the floor, usually into the waiting arms of a "catcher."

Charismatic James Lee Grady feels that being slain in the Spirit is common today because it is a learned experience, a tradition passed down from some of the Pentecostal forerunners, including the late Kathryn Kuhlman. One observer of Kuhlman tells how she simply walked past a mass choir and row upon row dropped under the power of the Holy Spirit as she passed by.

Grady recalls how he personally stood many times in a line of people, waiting for a Pentecostal evangelist to anoint him or pray for healing. He claims that in almost every case the minister placed his hand on his forehead and began to nudge him backward. And one time, when he refused to go limp and fall into the catcher's arms, he was mildly rebuked by the evangelist for resisting the Spirit.

There is absolutely no precedence in Scripture for this practice of falling down, or being slain in the Spirit. Falling to the floor in a swoon, real or pretend, simply has no connection with the believer being anointed or filled by the Spirit. If it is a matter of prostrating oneself before the Lord in order to show true remorse for sins and humbleness of spirit as one approaches God for mercy—that is the individual believer's prerogative.

Holy laughter

In an article appearing in the December 1994 *Calcedon Report,* Joseph R. McAuliffe reports on what he considers to be the latest rage sweeping across the charismatic landscape in this country as well as in England, Europe, Australia, Singapore, Hong Kong, and Latin America. It's called the laughter revival. In all fairness, we must note that this phenomenon is controversial among charismatics and that not all regard it as a bona fide gift of the Spirit. And like all charismatic phenomena, it appears in various forms, and each congregation that uses it will restrict its use in conformity to its practice.

In the spring of 1993, a South African evangelist named Rodney Howard-Browne began a week of revival meetings that launched the contemporary laughter movement. Howard-Browne's messages are centered on the believer being filled with the Holy Spirit. McAuliffe reports that despite holding five-hour meetings, Howard-Browne rarely completes a sermon; he is constantly interrupted by the unusual activities that take place, especially the laughter.[12]

The evangelist claims that this unusual emotional response of uncontrolled laughter—and sometimes uncontrolled weeping—is a manifestation of the Holy Spirit's presence. When the evangelist touches people on the forehead, many of them will fall to the floor giggling, sometimes for hours. Howard-Browne himself experienced the "holy laughter" after he gave the Holy Spirit a desperate ultimatum: "Either you come down here and touch me, or I will come up there and touch you."[13]

In the summer of 1997, Howard-Browne held a series of revival meetings in Fort Worth, Texas. Jim Jones, a reporter for the Fort Worth *Star-Telegram,* described what he saw at one of the meetings:

> A woman laughed uncontrollably. A man leapt from a front pew of the church and began spasmodically jerking, his arms flying up and down. [The evangelist's response to these interruptions was:] "In the name of Jesus, let it bubble up. Let it bubble up out of your belly." . . . A young woman left her seat and began running and leaping around the sanctuary. About 20 others followed her as the congregation

applauded. A man in his late 20s who had been joining the others running through the church leaned on a back wall to rest, breathing heavily and still engaged in unbridled laughter. "Run only one way," Howard-Browne advised. Then he broke into a frenzy of laughter, left the lectern and ran up the center aisle of the church, laughing all the way.[14]

Julia Duin, writing in *Charisma* and *Christian Life* notes that Howard-Browne's followers have labeled him the harbinger of revival, while his critics label the raucous "holy laughter" that typically erupts in his huge meetings as "just one more charismatic fad."[15]

Holy Scripture has things to say about the conduct of those who lead the worship services and also about those who participate. These words still apply today: "Everything should be done in a fitting and orderly way" (1 Corinthians 14:40). "Guard your steps when you go to the house of God. Go near to listen rather than to offer the sacrifice of fools, who do not know that they do wrong" (Ecclesiastes 5:1). Unlike speaking in tongues and healing, there is nothing in Scripture that hints that anyone in the early church had this gift. Perhaps these words of the apostle Paul summarize the matter best: "Let the word of Christ dwell in you richly as you teach and admonish one another with all wisdom, and as you sing psalms, hymns and spiritual songs with gratitude in your hearts to God. And whatever you do, whether in word or deed, do it all in the name of the Lord Jesus, giving thanks to God the Father through him" (Colossians 3:16,17). These words stand in stark contrast to those who would foster "holy laughter," and they alone determine the tenor of God-pleasing worship.

Prosperity-faith and positive confession

The proponents of the prosperity-faith philosophy regard health and wealth as the right of every Christian, at least those who acquire enough faith to gain them.[16] This teaching also goes by the popular titles "name it–claim it" and "confess it–possess it" theology.

Another teaching is called positive confession. Proponents of this doctrine claim that anyone who makes a positive confession that God wants him to receive the blessing and who overcomes all doubt that God has already answered the prayer for faith has enough faith to acquire health and prosperity.[17]

Don Matzat thoroughly explores this strange and offensive theology of the charismatics:

> Probably the most popular and controversial teaching that is part of the charismatic movement is the "name and claim/health and wealth" teaching. This teaching is promoted by such popular charismatic figures as Kenneth Hagin (who has been most responsible for spreading this faith theology), Kenneth Copeland, Charles Capps, Marilyn Hickey, Oral Roberts, Robert Tilton, and Paul Yonggi Cho and is strongly believed by a large portion of charismatic/Pentecostal people.

> The "name and claim" teaching promotes faith as the active appropriation and "claiming" of the biblical promises of God. Joined to faith is the practice of affirmation or "positive confession" in which the desired blessing is confessed and positively affirmed. In the doctrine of the faith teachers, "confession equals possession." Some teachers, such as Cho, also teach the practice of visualization whereby the intended object of the faith and affirmation is visualized and such "vision" is held in the imagination until which time it comes into reality.

> For example, if I desired financial prosperity, according to this teaching I would stand upon or claim the promise of 3 John 2, "Dear friend, I pray that you may enjoy good health and that all may go well with you, even as your soul is getting along well," (a very important verse for the faith/prosperity teachers) and begin to verbally confess possession of prosperity or financial gain even before it comes into being. Such combination of faith, confession or affirmation, (plus visualization) allegedly brings into reality the intended result. For these teachers, man functions as God functions . . . and calls things that are not as if they were.

> Within the faith, positive confession movement there is no room for negatives, since negative confessions supposedly produce negative results. There are many charismatics who guard their words very cautiously, believing their words have creative power, producing what they confess. God

desires, according to this teaching, only positive blessings in our lives which should be confessed to be experienced.[18]

If it's wealth that you want, or a home or a new car, make your prayer to God and at the same time believe that you possess what you pray for, and even go so far as to confess or profess that you now own it, and you will have it. Dave Hunt, the author of *Beyond Seduction: A Return to Biblical Christianity,* gives an example of what "positive confession" amounts to: "If we pray for someone's healing and then confess that the individual is healed, there is no way that person cannot be healed. Consequently, we should not confess that they are sick, neither should we seek the help of a doctor (if a healing has not come), but should continue to confess the healing."[19]

With this "faith" theology in mind, the following remark is made: "The biblical teaching of *supplication* has been replaced by the idea that we can get God to do whatever we want to by following the rules of the game. . . . Some of the Positive Confession leaders not only admit but teach that the methods, laws, and principles they use are also used successfully by occultists."[20]

Not all who were once deeply involved in the faith theology have stayed with it. Jim Bakker, a well-known televangelist, was imprisoned for defrauding his followers. He had lived lavishly and espoused the health/wealth gospel. In his prison cell he studied the teachings of Jesus and came to the solid conclusion that the health/wealth gospel is wrong. In June 1992 he wrote a letter that his daughter mailed to his supporters. In it is a confession of wrongdoing. Here is a portion of what he had to say:

> Many today believe that the evidence of God's blessing on them is a new car, a new house, a good job, and riches, etc. But that is far from the truth of God's Word. Jesus did not teach that riches were a sign of God's blessings. In fact, Jesus said, "It is hard for a rich man to enter the Kingdom of Heaven." And he talked about the deceitfulness of riches.

> There is no way, if you take the whole counsel of God's Word, that you can equate riches or material things as a sign of God's blessing.

I have asked God to forgive me and I ask all who have sat under my ministry to forgive me for preaching a gospel emphasizing earthly prosperity. Jesus said, "Do not lay up for yourselves treasures on earth." He wants us to be in love with Him. If we equate earthly possessions and earthly relationships with God's favor, what do we tell the billions of those living in poverty, or what do you do if depression hits, or what do you say to those who lose a loved one?[21]

One more quotation will help put the matter into perspective. In *Pentecostals from the Inside Out,* one writer observes:

Nothing has prompted more debate within Pentecostal and charismatic circles over the last decade [the 1980s] than the controversy over faith healing and Christian prosperity. Nicknamed by detractors as the "health-and-wealth!" or "name it-claim it" gospel, the "word-of-faith" movement has successfully captured a vocal segment of the growing charismatic revival. Though the specific number of adherents is not known, it features some of the charismatic movement's most powerful evangelists and largest multi-media ministries. The battlefield that has developed in the wake of this growth has threatened both the identity and the unity of the twentieth-century charismatic renewal.[22]

Inner, or soul, healing

The idea behind inner healing is that a person can call upon Jesus to go back with him in time, perhaps to his childhood, and if he has suffered some emotional hurt, Jesus can free him from its effect.[23] J. I. Packer explains it as "a counseling technique of leading pained, grieved, inhibited, and embittered souls to visualize Christ and involve him therapeutically in the reliving of their traumatic hurts, as a means to inner healing."[24]

Don Matzat claims that inner, or soul, healing is a very popular charismatic ministry, and he has written a book on the subject.[25] After extensive research, he has concluded that soul healing is based upon the mystical experiences offered in Jungian psychology.

Just how far this teaching can be taken is illustrated by the claims of Rita Bennett, the widow of Father Dennis Bennett, the "father" of the modern charismatic movement. She states that through the technique of mystical visualization, the "real" Jesus is present, healing people as he did while he walked the earth. Furthermore, she believes that even an unbeliever can receive inner healing through this visualized encounter with the real Jesus. Matzat labels such a claim as a classic example of false religious enthusiasm. Such people rest upon the flimsy foundations of reason and imagination to assure them of victory over the devil's power.[26]

Exorcism

Since Jesus and the disciples cast out demons, charismatics feel this should be an important part of their ministry. In *Pentecostals from the Inside Out*, one of the authors reminds us that the charismatic renewal has brought with it an emphasis on demons. He reports that some of the mainline denominational charismatics regularly practice exorcisms, noting one charismatic Lutheran church that has a minister on staff who specializes in exorcising demons. "The extreme fringe who hold to the belief have gone so far as to attribute almost any difficulty Christians experience to demonic control. Some of it is so ludicrous that it is funny (a demon of fingernail biting, for example)."[27] Charismatic leaders have been known to accuse those who disagree with their teachings, or who question their authority, of being demon possessed.

Many charismatics carry on ministries based on "power encounters," using so-called miracles to overcome resistance to the gospel. Exorcising demons is a favorite power encounter with many. In fact, some charismatic ministers and evangelists make exorcising demons their chief activity. Needless to say, they manage to find "demons" under every rock and behind every bush.

Edward N. Gross in *Miracles, Demons, and Spiritual Warfare: An Urgent Call for Discernment,* sums up the matter: "I think this is an unhealthy and imbalanced approach to spiritual warfare. It is simply unbiblical. The inspired teaching of Paul mentions prayer much, but exorcism little."[28]

Empire building and authoritarianism

The desire to have authority over others and even to build personal empires is part of our sinful nature. Numerous examples can be found of how church leaders have misused their authority and built little kingdoms for themselves.

In the charismatic world, there is even more opportunity for this to happen. Leaders speak in tongues, have the gift of direct revelation from God, and can perform healings. This is a setup for disaster, and charismatics have had perhaps more than their share.

A God-pleasing method of governing has not been the rule in most charismatic churches, particularly independent ones. Since the renewal blossomed in the late 1960s, many groups degenerated quickly into legalism and authoritarianism. Many cases of "empire building" among big-name charismatics have been brought to the public's attention by the media.

There has been a backlash in many charismatic churches against the empire building and authoritarianism of their leaders. James Lee Grady reports: "Charismatics today are getting tired of the kingdom-building and personality-driven ministry. We are less prone to being dragged around to fulfill someone else's so-called 'vision'. We are more leery of wasting God's money on monuments to the flesh, and weary of being manipulated into being part of someone else's hidden agenda."[29]

These are some of the aberrations that have surfaced in the Pentecostal/charismatic movement. In the next chapter we will discuss two more, which are potentially more dangerous than the ones we have just examined.

.

8

LACK OF DOCTRINAL CLARITY
AND ECUMENISM

Lack of doctrinal clarity

The doctrinal emphasis of the Pentecostal/charismatic movement has been on the person, work, fruit, and gifts of the Holy Spirit. Pentecostals and charismatics believe they must offset what they see as the lack of emphases on these teachings in the past. Renewing the church and evangelizing the world are their two main goals, and they conclude that these goals can be reached if each charismatic group remains true to its own teachings, experiences the Holy Spirit baptism, and enjoys the use of charismatic gifts.

Agreement in doctrine on the basis of carefully thought out and carefully worded statements is simply not a priority with the charismatics. One of the writers of *Welcome, Holy Spirit: A Study of Charismatic Renewal in the Church* admits, "The

charismatic renewal has not addressed itself to doctrinal formulation in a comprehensive or systematic way. Rather, in
keeping with its nature as a movement, it has stressed certain
truths that appear to have been neglected in the church or
developed in a one-sided way."[1]

On the other hand, much emphasis is placed on the use of
the Holy Spirit's gifts in making the gospel attractive to the
people who are being evangelized. W. Dennis Pederson writes
in *International Lutheran Renewal*:

> The primary purpose of renewal is to present the person,
> work, gifts, fruit and power of the Holy Spirit to the pastors
> and lay people in our churches. We charismatics are to be
> apologists for the Holy Spirit. No other purpose fits us
> because outside of our personal encounter with the Holy
> Spirit, which is our common experience, we have no founda-
> tion out of which to build any house—personal, family, con-
> gregational or worldwide. Our common base is the fact that
> we have been encountered by the Holy Spirit in a personal
> way. The purpose of the charismatic renewal as a whole is to
> facilitate the release of the Holy Spirit. It is a mission of
> renewal in the Holy Spirit that we are about. The charis-
> matic renewal is a free movement of "baptized in the Holy
> Spirit" Christians who, out of love for the Lord and the
> church seek to be incarnational vessels for the release of the
> Spirit into the lives of other people. The mission of renewal
> includes evangelization in the power of the Holy Spirit, with
> signs and wonders following.[2]

Charismatic ecumenism

The lack of doctrinal emphasis gives the charismatic movement a natural affinity with the ecumenical movement. The
ecumenical movement has as its goal to unite all the denominations of Christendom. It attempts to arrive at its goal not by
bringing about doctrinal agreement, but by overlooking agreement in doctrine and substituting for it a general gospel or
some social issue.

To some extent, the ecumenical movement in its traditional
sense has lost steam. As one writer put it, "Ecumenism is yes-
terday's idea and is widely seen as a spent force. . . . Who
cares about the World Council of Churches?"[3]

In spite of this assessment, let us not think that the ecumenical movement is dead, shriveled, and ready to blow away. The charismatics and Pentecostals have proven to be a force to be reckoned with on the ecumenical front.

When the charismatic renewal first came on the scene in the early 1960s, there was considerable contact across denominational lines, and this continued well into the 1970s. The charismatics soon became convinced that they had found the theological happening that all sides could hold in common: the baptism in the Holy Spirit and its manifestation of charismatic gifts, especially the gift of glossolalia. The issue from the start was not "What doctrines do you bring to the movement?" but rather "We both share the same powerful experience. What could be more important than that—at least as long as we all confess Jesus as Savior and Lord?"

In his book *In the Latter Days: The Outpouring of the Holy Spirit in the Twentieth Century*, Vinson Synan expresses the matter rather bluntly: "My major viewpoint is that there is only one outpouring of the Holy Spirit in the latter days, although the streams flow through channels known as 'classical Pentecostalism,' Protestant 'neo-Pentecostalism,' and the 'Catholic charismatic renewal.' In the end it adds up to one great historical phenomenon which has had a profound effect on Christianity around the world."[4]

Charismatic conferences have been a main vehicle for ecumenical expression. For example, the first international conference on the Holy Spirit, which was held at Minneapolis in 1972, concluded with a Communion service in which all "born-again believers" were invited to participate. Speakers included Father Edward D. O'Connor, a professor at Notre Dame University and a leading figure in the Catholic charismatic renewal.

In an article by Larry Christenson in the *Lutheran Charismatic Renewal Newsletter* of July 1977, this Lutheran charismatic leader does some reminiscing about charismatic conferences he has been a part of:

> From the beginning Lutherans have maintained a strong sense of the ecumenical nature of the charismatic renewal. We always include speakers from other traditions at the

International Lutheran Conference on the Holy Spirit. A high point at the 1976 conference came when Pastor Donald Pfotenhauer, grandson of the former president of the Lutheran Church—Missouri Synod, publicly confessed "our sins and the sins of our fathers against our Roman Catholic brethren," and asked forgiveness of Leon Joseph Cardinal Suenens, a featured speaker of the evening. Cardinal Suenens responded in kind, saying that had the leaders of the Roman Catholic Church been "more patient and more Christian" they would not have treated Martin Luther in the shameful way they did.

Lutherans will be coming to the 1977 Conference in Kansas City with a keen sense of their calling to "labor among Lutherans"—to pray and work for charismatic renewal in their own immediate family. But they will also come *eager to rub shoulders with Christians across the whole spectrum of the charismatic renewal.* For it is true, as this enthusiastic charismatic pointed out to me, the Lutheran tradition embraces a variety that enables us to identify a broad spectrum of fellow believers. We are on tip toes to see what the Lord will do; and *with arms stretched out to touch hands with many brethren.*[5]

However, as the 1970s wore on, the ecumenical contact among charismatics began to diminish as charismatics, conscious of the need for renewal in their own denominational groups, turned most of their attention inward.[6] This focus continued on into the next decade. This diminished activity on the ecumenical front did not go unnoticed and unchallenged. Reverend Vinson Synan, chairman of the North American Renewal Service Committee and a leading ecumenist among the charismatics, recalls:

Charismatic leaders felt uneasy about this development. They sensed that the ecumenical dimension of the renewal was no frill or add-on. It was somehow critical to the Spirit's purpose and strategy. Had the time come to raise again the ecumenical question in the Charismatic Renewal? Might the worldwide Pentecostal/charismatic renewal be used to advance the cause of Christian unity, and the purpose of Christ?[7]

This question was raised by three men—Larry Christenson (Lutheran), Tom Forrest (Catholic), and Michael Harper (Anglican). It led to the convening of a small group of charismatics representing their three respective traditions. This group met several times over three years. In these meetings the group came under the conviction that the Pentecostal/charismatic renewal should make its focus for the 1990s carrying on world evangelization with the goal of presenting Jesus on his two thousandth birthday a world with an absolute majority of Christians. From 1983 to 1988, during which time their proposal was publicized, more and more charismatic leaders joined in support of a "decade of evangelization." Finally, just outside ancient Jerusalem, 108 Pentecostal and charismatic leaders gathered the week of Pentecost 1989, for the purpose of praying for a new outpouring of the Holy Spirit. Thirty-one nations were represented.

> The week was filled with prayer, praise, and challenging messages on the Great Commission. Participants came from a wide spectrum of Christian denominations: Catholic, Protestant, Pentecostal, Nondenominational . . . In the progress of the vigil, a specific proposal was put forward to convene a World Renewal Leaders Conference on World Evangelization for the summer of 1991.[8]

The 1991 conference was attended by more than two thousand renewal leaders in Brighton, England. In the words of one of the organizers, Larry Christenson: "The men and women who gather together in Brighton this summer are a living epistle, a divine statement concerning unity among Christians in the task of world evangelization. . . . They come expecting the working of the Holy Spirit by which the unity that exists in God himself shall be found in them . . . 'that the world may believe.'"[9] And so, in a grand ecumenical venture, fostered by recognized charismatic leaders from all over the world, the Pentecostals and charismatics have bound themselves together—Catholics, Protestants, Nondenominationalists—for the purpose of worldwide evangelization.

The headship, or lordship, of Christ is another basis for the strong spirit of ecumenism that drives the charismatics. The charismatics point to two passages of Scripture in particular. "Just as each of us has one body with many members, and these members do not all have the same function, so in Christ we who are many form one body, and each member belongs to all the others" (Romans 12:4,5). "There is one body and one Spirit—just as you were called to one hope when you were called—one Lord, one faith, one baptism; one God and Father of all, who is over all and through all and in all" (Ephesians 4:4-6). Paul Anderson writes in *International Lutheran Renewal*: "Unity in the body of Christ is a command, not an option. The ecumenical movement had shown some signs of effeteness [of being outmoded] through its decades of efforts. The charismatic renewal came along and seemed to demonstrate a unity trans-denominationally with surprising ease, *by appreciating* the differences and exalting the common Lord."[10]

We can summarize three goals of the charismatics that show how important it is that their movement become thoroughly ecumenical.

The first goal is to heal the body of Christ through renewal. The Geneva Conference, which was held March 8 to 13, 1980, named the following as elements of a renewed and unified church, calling them marks of the church in the New Testament:

> A new openness toward the healing power and lordship of Jesus . . . renewal of spiritual life of the church in its local congregations . . . spontaneity, openness, freedom, and joy in praise and worship . . . new interest in the Bible as God's living Word . . . a deeper experience of the reality, holiness and transcendence of God . . . deeper interest and new openness in regard to the essential doctrines of the Trinity, the divinity of Christ, his death and resurrection, confirmed in experience . . . renewal of the service of healing for the sick . . . lay leadership . . . new incentive for evangelization, missions, and witness in the power of the Spirit.[11]

The second goal is a unified front to enhance evangelism. Charismatics want to demonstrate the unity of Christ's body so as to produce a powerful witness to the unchurched. Many people are turned off to the Christian religion because of the number of different denominations. The number of denominations and the variations even within denominations have a tendency to confuse and overwhelm the unchurched.

The third goal is a gigantic evangelism thrust. Many in the charismatic renewal believe that if the world really is to be evangelized, the work must be done especially by Pentecostal/charismatic Christians. After all, they have the zeal for it, and they can employ their "power encounters" to help non-Christians decide for Christ.

Present-day charismatics regard their Holy Spirit baptism as an endowment to help them accomplish the evangelization of the world. In what it will take to get this job done—the spirit of joyful worship and enthusiasm for evangelizing the world, and the heady power of speaking in tongues and healing—there are no theological boundaries.

Part Three

THE PENTECOSTAL/CHARISMATIC

MOVEMENT

IN THE LIGHT OF SCRIPTURE

9

SCRIPTURAL BAPTISM OF THE SPIRIT

In the first two parts of this book, we outlined the history and doctrines of the Pentecostal/charismatic movement, in particular the doctrine about spiritual gifts.

We turn now to an analysis of this movement. The main questions we will be asking are (1) Do the gifts as they are understood and practiced in these movements line up with the gifts the early church received as described in Scripture? (2) Are the doctrines of these movements taught in Scripture?

Before we begin with this analysis, we must point out that we believe that all those who confess Jesus as their Savior from sin are members of God's holy Christian church. Pentecostals and charismatics confess this truth. Pentecostals and charismatics who believe this truth are fellow heirs of God's eternal kingdom.

What we are addressing in this section are what we believe to be false teachings and false spirits that have invaded the church through these movements. We are convinced that the teachings of this movement undermine the central teaching of Christianity—justification by faith alone—and therefore pose a threat to the faith of those inside the movement.

The Holy Spirit comes through scriptural Baptism to regenerate and renew sinners

In the historical part, we noted an intense desire on the part of John Wesley to become holy. Based on his own experience, he taught that any Christian can experience what he called Christian perfection. In this state a Christian becomes free from the struggle against sin that Paul describes in Romans 7.

We traced the history of this teaching on American soil. There it gave rise to a series of revivals, or times when God supposedly was pouring out his Spirit. The Spirit was giving Christians a "second blessing," or a "baptism of the Spirit," distinct from water Baptism, which gave them an instantaneous power over sin and growth in sanctification. The desire for revival and power over sin reached a high point in the 1890s in the holiness movement of the Methodist church. In a fevered pitch, the holiness movement created a yearning for the Holy Spirit. This yearning finally resolved itself in the Pentecostal movement, which spilled over into mainline denominations in what we call the charismatic movement.

All these groups wanted a greater infilling of the Spirit than they received at conversion. At the heart of these movements is an experience they call "the baptism of the Holy Spirit," a powerful spiritual experience accompanied by strong emotional feelings and signs, most notably speaking in tongues.

Is "second blessing theology" scriptural? Let's examine what the Bible says.

Filled with the Holy Spirit, the apostle Peter preached a powerful sermon to the unbelieving Jews on Pentecost Sunday. Incisively, he laid out before them their sin of rejecting the Son of God. The Holy Spirit worked through Peter's words with the result that a large number of hearers were convicted in their hearts of having committed terrible sins against Christ.

What were they to do in order to escape the judgment of God? Peter urged them to repent, that is, to turn from their sins, and he immediately offered them the Sacrament of Holy Baptism: "Repent and be baptized, every one of you, in the name of Jesus Christ for the forgiveness of your sins. And you will receive the gift of the Holy Spirit. The promise is for you and your children and for all who are far off—for all whom the Lord our God will call" (Acts 2:38,39).

Peter's hearers were to be baptized in the name of the very person they had previously rejected. They were to be forgiven and saved from their sins by the very blood they had caused to be spilled on the cross when they called for Christ's crucifixion. *Name* refers to everything that the name-bearer is. Baptism in the name of Jesus Christ seals the sinner with Jesus' name, thus joining him to all that Christ is and to all that Christ has done for mankind through his sinless life and death. Christ was the perfect, once-for-all payment to God for the whole world's sins. Simply put, the person who is joined to Jesus Christ in Baptism has his sins forgiven.

It is through faith that the sinner accepts God's offer of forgiveness of sins in Baptism. Yes, through faith he clings to the precious name of Jesus Christ, embracing with his heart the Savior and all that he did to purchase mankind's salvation.

Note carefully Peter's words. He very clearly states that the gift of the Holy Spirit is received in Baptism. The Holy Spirit comes to the person to move his heart to believe, to be joined to Christ to receive forgiveness for his sins and to receive all Christ's benefits. The Holy Spirit was at work as Peter preached his Pentecost message. The people were humbled before God through Peter's message; their hearts were terrorized by his reminder of how they had sinned. Led by the Holy Spirit, they gladly accepted God's offer of Baptism. Then, when they were baptized, they were sealed in Christ, and the Spirit put into their hearts the faith to accept the remission of sins. Three thousand souls received Baptism and with it—according to the promise made to them—the gift of the Holy Spirit.

In his letter to the Ephesians, Paul gives us insight as to how the Holy Spirit works faith in human hearts through Baptism. The apostle calls Baptism "the washing with water *through the word*" (5:26). Thus the Word—the name of Christ, the name of the Father, and the name of the Holy Spirit together with all God's promises—joins the water to form the means of grace by which the Holy Spirit imparts faith and forgiveness to the sinner. The water, the name of the triune God, and the word of divine promise come together to form the wonderful visible sign of forgiveness, Baptism.

Consider Jesus' own words concerning Baptism. One night a man named Nicodemus visited him in order to satisfy his curiosity about Jesus' teachings and miracles. Jesus seized the opportunity to set this member of the Jewish ruling council straight concerning this question: How does the sinner enter God's kingdom? In the process our Lord also taught Nicodemus how the sinner turns from a life of sin to a life of serving God with a holy life. Jesus answered Nicodemus: "I tell you the truth, no one can enter the kingdom of God unless he is born of water and the Spirit. Flesh gives birth to flesh, but the Spirit gives birth to spirit" (John 3:5,6).

"Flesh gives birth to flesh" means that flesh, which is full of sin and has no good thing dwelling in it, can only give birth to the same. Through *physical* birth a person becomes a member of the sinful human race. When he leaves his mother's womb and enters the world, he possesses physical life. Nevertheless, he is born *dead*, for he enters the world in a condition of *spiritual* deadness. Indeed—a person is born alive, yet at the same time is dead. It is possible to live out one's days on earth, even to a ripe old age, in the natural state of *spiritual* deadness. But without spiritual rebirth, or regeneration, a person cannot be fit for the kingdom of God, and upon physical death he will enter the horrors of a final and eternal separation from God. This is known as eternal death. Jesus' words to Nicodemus were, "No one can enter the kingdom of God unless he is born of water and the Spirit" (John 3:5). Unless a person is born again spiritually—that is, brought to faith in Christ—he simply cannot be saved from his sins and enter heaven.

Plainly, the rebirth that Jesus calls for takes place through Baptism and is brought about by the Holy Spirit. When Nicodemus asked how it is possible for a man when he is old to be born a second time, Jesus told him how such a thing comes about: by being "born of water and the Spirit" (John 3:5). The expression "water and Spirit" is a comprehensive one and simply refers to Baptism. Wonderfully, the Holy Spirit joins himself to scriptural Baptism, working through what God has promised and what the water in this sacred rite now signifies—the washing away of sins. The result of being baptized is that the person is given faith in Jesus Christ, or is sealed in the faith he may already have from hearing the gospel message. The Holy Spirit also places the confession "I believe in Jesus Christ as my Lord and Savior" on the baptized person's lips. Furthermore, the Holy Spirit, having been given as a gift in Baptism, lives in the believer to keep him in the faith and to keep him confessing Christ with his lips. The believer has the Holy Spirit!

Paul wrote to Titus: "He saved us, not because of righteous things we had done, but because of his mercy. He saved us through the washing of *rebirth and renewal by the Holy Spirit*" (3:5,6). Plainly, Paul reminded Titus that the washing of Baptism results in spiritual rebirth and renewal, which then saves the person from damnation. The result of being baptized is to be no longer spiritually dead and unbelieving, but to be spiritually alive and believing. No longer simply "flesh born of flesh," he is now "spirit born of Spirit." His new man, the result of his rebirth and renewal, believes in Christ, and he is saved through this faith.

The theology of Pentecostalism simply does not understand, appreciate, or represent accurately the scriptural concept of Baptism and how the Holy Spirit is connected with it. To begin with, the Pentecostals regard Baptism as *something the person does, as an act of obedience and sacrifice on the believer's part toward God*:

> Thus in water baptism, *which is an action from our side, we* seal God's trustworthiness, and in the Spirit-baptism, *which is an action from God's side, he* places the seal upon our sincerity, the sincerity which we have brought to him.

Water baptism is the rite of entrance into the Christian church, and symbolizes *spiritual life begun*; . . . Water baptism in itself *has no saving power*; people are baptized not in order to be saved but because they are saved. Therefore we cannot say that the rite is absolutely essential to salvation. *But we may insist that it is essential to full obedience.*[1]

This quotation is fairly representative of what many in the Reformed branch of Christianity say about Baptism. They say that the Spirit cannot come through baptizing with water. They say he cannot use an outward sign: water in connection with God's Word.

The Pentecostal doctrine does not conform to any of the passages of Holy Scripture that speak of the saving power of Baptism and the relation of the Holy Spirit to it.

Baptism and sanctification

At the heart of Pentecostal teaching is a desire for holiness. This is not hard to understand. Once the charismatic has shut himself off from Baptism as a means of grace (and for that matter the Word of God also—at least in theory), he has nowhere to turn. When he experiences his own lack of sanctification, he yearns for the Spirit, but his theology provides him with no answer other than some sort of direct working of the Spirit.

In Scripture, God's gracious forgiveness of sins is always front and center. Sanctification is always bound to forgiveness; it is always the way the forgiven sinner responds to his gracious God. Scripture teaches that when the Christian remembers his Baptism, he remembers how God has forgiven him and how he should live as a child of God. So the Spirit works in Baptism to lead the Christian to a greater degree of sanctification.

Paul wrote powerfully on this matter in his letter to the Romans. There he reminds all believers:

What shall we say, then? Shall we go on sinning so that grace may increase? By no means! We died to sin; how can we live in it any longer? Or don't you know that all of us who were baptized into Christ Jesus were baptized into his death? We were therefore buried with him through baptism into death in order that, just as Christ was raised from the dead through the glory of the Father, we too may live a new life. . . . offer yourselves to God, as those who have been brought from death to life. . . . You have been set free from sin and have become slaves to righteousness (6:1-4,13,18).

Paul thus reminds us of a wonderful and comforting truth: the Holy Spirit, who regenerates and renews the sinner through faith, continues to work in the baptized believer's life so that he is able to shun sin and live a holy life to God's glory. The Holy Spirit, who inspired the above words, demonstrates that he wants to use the believer's Baptism as a constant reminder of the new, holy life he is to live daily for God. The Holy Spirit reminds the believer that in Baptism his sins were washed away, he died to sin, and he became alive to God. This means that with the Holy Spirit's power in him, the believer should daily crucify his sin-loving flesh and with his new, spiritual nature serve righteousness.

Paul E. Kretzmann points out that "regeneration is a single act, but the renewing thus begun by the Holy Ghost continues throughout the life of the Christian. The new spiritual creature wrought or created in Baptism is renewed from day to day" (2 Corinthians 4:16; 1 Peter 4:1).[2] This continual renewing of the believer can only be accomplished by the Holy Spirit, who has been given to him in Baptism. "We were all *baptized by one Spirit* into one body—whether Jews or Greeks, slave or free—and we were all *given the one Spirit to drink*" (1 Corinthians 12:13). The baptized believer has the Holy Spirit, who is active in the believer's day-to-day life, helping him shun sin and live righteously to God's glory by his new spiritual nature.

The charismatic or Pentecostal, having shut himself off from the means of grace, awaits a direct outpouring of the Holy Spirit. Since he does not confess the power of Baptism, he cannot ask God to give him the Spirit and then go to the source of the Spirit, which is the gospel in Word and sacraments.

What is it like to receive the Spirit?

Scripture also speaks about what it is like to receive the Holy Spirit, that is, what characteristics the Christian displays that make him sure of the Spirit.

Pentecostals and charismatics want this kind of evidence. Remember, that was Charles Parham's challenge to his students. Find out how Scripture says you are to know you have received the Spirit. They concluded it was by speaking in tongues. Wanting evidence is not wrong, but when a person's mind is turned in the direction of power to do miracles or speak in tongues, such evidence is usually slanted in a direction that is at odds with Scripture.

There is no doubt that one of the evidences of the Holy Spirit is the array of gifts God gives people in the church. At this point we are not going to argue that things like speaking in tongues and healing cannot be evidence that a person has the Spirit—even in these modern times. Certainly that was the case in the early church. We will discuss that issue in future chapters. Now we merely want to look at some passages of Scripture that will concentrate on what Scripture considers the basic and most important evidence of the Spirit: faith in Christ.

Paul wrote this word of instruction to the Corinthian Christians: "No one who is speaking by the Spirit of God says, 'Jesus be cursed,' and no one can say, 'Jesus is Lord,' except by the Holy Spirit" (1 Corinthians 12:3). If a person is not connected to the Holy Spirit, he will repudiate the gospel of Christ; if he does not do so in public, he will certainly do it in his heart. But when a person has the Holy Spirit in him, he will be led to confess, from the heart and with his mouth, that Jesus is Lord. For the mouth eventually reveals what the heart conceals.

The Corinthian Christians pursued spiritual gifts, especially the supernatural ones. But what if they did not receive these gifts? They had the Holy Spirit, nonetheless, for they confessed Christ to be their Lord and Savior. They did not need the presence of supernatural gifts as evidence of their possession of the Spirit. If they confessed Jesus as Lord, that was itself the primary evidence. To know what a blessing of the Holy Spirit this simple confession of faith in Christ is, the Corinthians needed only to recall how they once had lived. Formerly they had worshiped dumb idols. But when they learned to call Jesus "Lord," they were graciously delivered from that. And they did so by the power of the Holy Spirit.

Paul has this comforting word of assurance: "Having believed, you were marked in him with a seal, the promised Holy Spirit, who is a deposit guaranteeing our inheritance" (Ephesians 1:13,14). Is the Spirit in us believers? Yes. Spiritually speaking, we were offspring of the devil, children of wrath (2:3). But in Baptism, God marked us with a seal, the promised Holy Spirit, and identified us as his own children by faith in Christ. Now we stand to inherit everlasting life. While we do not enjoy heaven at the present time, we nevertheless have the down payment on it, the guarantee that heaven is ours. "The Holy Spirit in us" is that down payment, that guarantee. How do we know we have the Spirit? Our Baptism, the faith we now have, the confession our lips make, together with the wonderful hope of heaven that fills our minds and hearts—these are the powerful evidences.

The Holy Spirit enables us to experience God's love in Christ

Saint Paul writes, "We rejoice in the hope of the glory of God. Not only so, but we also rejoice in our sufferings, because we know that suffering produces perseverance; perseverance, character; and character, hope. And hope does not disappoint us, because God has poured out his love into our hearts by the Holy Spirit, whom he has given us" (Romans 5:2-5). How wonderful it is to have the hope of eternal life and glory with God in heaven and to have this hope especially when life is hard, such as in times of suffering. And it is not in any way a false hope. It will not disappoint us in the end. The basis of this hope is God's love for us, revealed in the sacrifice of his own dear Son on the cross for our sins. We also see evidence of God's love for us acted out in our lives in countless ways, especially in answering our prayers and thus providing us with the help, comfort, and strengthening we often need.

Do we know this love? Then we can be sure the Holy Spirit is working in us. The Holy Spirit has poured out God's love into our hearts. He made us aware of God's love; he led us to trust it; he continues to use it to draw us back and to comfort us when we sin. At other times when seemingly there is no hope, he gives us hope through God's love. We know we have the Holy Spirit in us when we experience the presence of his love in our hearts by faith and rejoice in the hope he has given us in Christ: hope for this life and, best of all, hope for the life to come.

The Holy Spirit testifies that we are children of God

Paul gives this important reminder to all believers: "Those who are led by the Spirit of God are sons of God. For you did not receive a spirit that makes you a slave again to fear, but you received the Spirit of sonship. And by him we cry, 'Abba, Father.' The Spirit himself testifies with our spirit that we are God's children" (Romans 8:14-16).

The Spirit does not fill us with fear by leading us back to the demands of the law but gives us boldness to call God our Father by leading us to Christ! And so we go to God in time of need, saying to him: "Father, I bring to you my hurts, my disappointments, and my wants. Please help me, heal me, comfort me. I bring my sins to you. Here they are. I confess them. Please pardon me."

This Christian way of talking to God is wonderful evidence of the Spirit within us, who testifies to our own spirit that we are God's children, who have the right to approach God with utmost confidence. We have not received a spirit of slavery that makes us afraid of God or drives us to obey him out of blind panic. We want to do what is right because we have the Holy Spirit in us leading us with the assurance that we are the beloved children of a loving heavenly Father.

Through the Holy Spirit we produce the fruit of righteousness

In his day Paul never expected any individual Christian to have this or that miraculous gift. But he did urge all Christians to walk in step with the Spirit who lived in them.

He wrote: "The fruit of the Spirit is love, joy, peace, patience, kindness, goodness, faithfulness, gentleness and self-control. . . . Those who belong to Christ Jesus have crucified the sinful nature with its passions and desires. Since we live by the Spirit, let us keep in step with the Spirit. Let us not become conceited, provoking and envying each other" (Galatians 5:22-26).

Whenever the apostles tell Christians to serve God in righteousness, they are not exhorting Christians to seek a "baptism" in the Spirit. Rather, they are speaking to people who have already received the Holy Spirit in the Sacrament of Baptism, with the result that they have died to sin and are now alive to righteousness. The apostles are therefore urging good works among a people set apart to God who are fully capable of performing them. And so the fruit of righteousness, or good works, that we believers produce in our everyday lives is evidence that the Spirit lives and is powerfully working within us.

The Holy Spirit and prayer

Paul instructed the Christians to "pray in the Spirit on all occasions with all kinds of prayers and requests. With this in mind, be alert and always keep on praying for all the saints. Pray also for me" (Ephesians 6:18,19).

Prayer is an act of faith and as such can be carried on only in connection with the Holy Spirit in us. The Spirit reminds us to pray, shows us what things to pray for, and convinces us that God will hear our prayers for Jesus' sake. To "pray in the Spirit on all occasions with all kinds of prayers and requests" means that the Holy Spirit is in us continually and that he continually helps us with our prayers.

This activity within us is additional proof of the Holy Spirit's presence.

The Holy Spirit in us gives us love for others

The apostle John reminds us: "No one has ever seen God; but if we love one another, God lives in us and his love is made complete in us. We know that we live in him and he in us, because he has given us of his Spirit. And so we know and

147

rely on the love God has for us. God is love. Whoever lives in love lives in God, and God in him" (1 John 4:12,13,16).

In his *Sixth Homily,* the ancient church father Augustine explains these words of John and reminds us of the importance of love as evidence of the indwelling of the Holy Spirit:

> If then the witness of the presence of the Holy Ghost be not now given through these miracles, by what is it given, by what does one get to know that he has received the Holy Ghost? Let him question his own heart. If he love his brother, the Spirit of God dwelleth in him. Let him see, let him prove himself before the eyes of God, let him see whether there be in him the love of peace and unity, the love of the Church that is spread over the whole earth.[3]

When we search our hearts and find there the kind of love that God requires of his children and that he inspires in them through his love, we can be sure we have the Holy Spirit living in us.

Through Baptism the Holy Spirit has made us members of the church

Paul wrote, "We were all baptized by one Spirit into one body—whether Jews or Greeks, slave or free—and we were all given the one Spirit to drink" (1 Corinthians 12:13). In these words, Paul compares the Christian church to a human body. The believers are the members of the body; Christ is the head. How did we, who were dead in sin, become members of Christ's body? By the operation of the Holy Spirit in Baptism. In that holy rite, the Spirit brought us to faith, washed away our sins with Jesus' blood, and set us apart from the world by joining us to Christ. Since the Holy Spirit remains in his believers, we are continually nurtured in our spirit by his grace, for "we were all given the one Spirit to drink." Instead of urging his readers to experience a "baptism" in the Holy Spirit, the apostle Paul assured them that through Baptism they had already been baptized by the Holy Spirit and brought into membership of the church.

Be filled with the Spirit

Jesus instructs us, "If you then, though you are evil, know how to give good gifts to your children, how much more will your Father in heaven give the Holy Spirit to those who ask him!" (Luke 11:13). To ask God for the Holy Spirit to be given to us is to ask him to give us a fuller measure of the Spirit or, as one person put it, to enable the Spirit to have his way in our hearts.

The Spirit converted, quickened, enlightened, regenerated, and renewed us. He did all this by bringing us to faith in Christ. There is a continuing need for the Holy Spirit's infilling, a need for us to be renewed in the realization that we are sinful and that God has given us a Savior. Living a Christian life, as opposed to one of drunkenness and other flagrant sins, is made possible by the Holy Spirit's filling us with his presence and the power of his grace.

It is true that not all Christians are filled with the Holy Spirit to the same degree. Some are much stronger than others in their faith. Some fill their lives with more good works than others. Some know and understand God's Word more profoundly than others. Some possess a deeper brotherly love than others. Some are better at warding off temptation than others. But one thing is certain: all of us need to pray that God continually give us his Spirit. Thus Paul urges all believers: "Do not get drunk on wine, which leads to debauchery. Instead, be filled with the Spirit" (Ephesians 5:18).

A Pentecostal-type infilling?

There is no place in Scripture where God reveals to us that subsequent to Baptism there is a second blessing, or baptism in the Holy Spirit, that Christians are to seek. All emphasis is on the initial filling of the Spirit that took place in Baptism and on the ongoing filling of the Spirit that takes place when Christians are gathered around the Word and receive God's forgiveness in the Lord's Supper.

Being filled with the Spirit and producing the fruit of the Spirit constitutes an ongoing program of sanctification for every Christian. It is not a legitimate conclusion that the "garden variety" Christian does not have the Holy Spirit living in him in a personal way and empowering him for acts of Christian service. And it is certainly not true that Christians who have not had a Pentecostal-type experience are second-class Christians.

We need to be filled with the Spirit. But the Spirit we need to be filled with is the Spirit of Christ, the Spirit who teaches us to call God our Father and teaches us how we can do so. We need to be filled with that Spirit who teaches why we should use our bodies to serve the Lord and not ourselves, why we are truly slaves of righteousness and have every reason to avoid falling back into slavery to sin.

There is only one way to receive that Spirit, and that is by going to where Christ can be found—his Word and Sacraments. To reject those means and go casting about for some other source of spiritual life is a dangerous thing. For a Christian to become so frustrated with his lack of sanctification that he jettisons God's means of grace is to open himself to whatever other spirits there might be. The Pentecostal/charismatic spirit is just that—a willing substitute for the true Spirit of God.

There is nothing we need more than to grow in service to our Lord through the power of the Holy Spirit. But we must never settle for anything less than the true Spirit of God—given to us at Baptism, renewed in us through daily contrition and repentance, and at work in us through God's Word. To settle for any lesser spirit—no matter how fulfilling and powerful it may seem—is to invite spiritual harm.

10

THE SCRIPTURAL GIFT OF TONGUES

The Spirit misused or a false spirit?

In Chapter 9 we contrasted the Pentecostal/charismatic baptism in the Spirit with the way Scripture describes a Christian's coming to faith. We saw that they are different and that the baptism in the Spirit taught by the Pentecostals and charismatics cannot be derived from Scripture.

Before we continue with our comparison of Scripture and the Pentecostal/charismatic movement, we must address a very important and foundational issue: Is the spirit behind the Pentecostal/charismatic movement the Holy Spirit or a false spirit from some other source?

Those who disagree with the movement often argue in two different directions. For example, in dealing with speaking in tongues, they refer to Saint Paul's words to the Corinthians and encourage Pentecostals and charismatics to take Paul's advice. Side-by-side with this argument, they express the opinion that Pentecostals and charismatics are tapping into a false spirit.

The problem with this argument or, rather, with the simultaneous use of both of these arguments, is that the two arguments cannot be used at the same time. They are mutually exclusive. If I encourage a person to use a spiritual gift God has given him and not to abuse it, that is one thing. If I claim that someone has a false spirit, that is quite another. In the one case, I assume that the person I am talking with has the true Spirit, and in the other case, I am claiming he has a false spirit. I can deal with the first person by pointing him to Scripture and encouraging him to take Scripture's words to heart. In the second case, all I can do is encourage him to give up his false spirit.

If we assume that the Pentecostal/charismatic experience and the miraculous signs that accompany it come from the Spirit of God, then we should point Pentecostals and charismatics to Scripture and help them use their gifts in accordance with Scripture. Yet when we appeal to Scripture in that way, we are acknowledging that their gifts are true spiritual gifts bestowed by the Holy Spirit and that their teaching and practice about the availability and use of spiritual gifts is in line with Scripture. By pointing them to Scripture in this way, we are only saying that *how* they are using their spiritual gifts is wrong.

But can a confessional Lutheran put himself into that frame of mind? A noncharismatic who does that should immediately reassess his own spiritual life and ask whether he is dismissing gifts he should rather be praying for. For example, anyone who uses Paul's instructions to the Corinthians to help a charismatic correctly use the gift of tongues is validating that gift. At the very least, this should lead him to wonder whether his own church has wrongly been dismissing the gift of tongues by claiming that they passed out of use in the early church.

Of course, we don't judge whether something is true on experience, ours or someone else's. We must judge it on the basis of Scripture. In the case of the Pentecostal/charismatic movement, we must ask whether such gifts are consistent with what the early church practiced, and we must examine if such teachings line up with Scripture.

It is our conclusion that these movements have ingested a false spirit and that this false spirit manifests itself in many aspects of the religious life of Pentecostals and charismatics. As we move forward in this book and look at how Scripture describes the gifts of the Spirit, we will come to the same conclusion that we came to in the previous chapter on Spirit baptism. The Pentecostal/charismatic gifts come from another spirit, just as their second blessing, "spirit baptism," does. We will use Scripture to help us understand the true nature of spiritual gifts and to show that the practice and teaching of the Pentecostal/charismatic movement is not in line with Scripture.

One more point before we continue. We wish to underline something we said at the beginning of the last chapter. When we say that the movements are generated by a false spirit, we are not denying that the true Spirit of God may very well be working in these people's hearts through the gospel. All who confess their sins and believe in Christ as Savior are members of God's church and possess the true Spirit of God, share in his gifts, and will inherit eternal life. What we are objecting to and exposing is the spiritual baggage they have taken on themselves by being associated with this movement and another—a false—spirit associated with it. If people have come to faith in the context of this movement—and we have no doubt that many have—then we rejoice and consider them brothers and sisters in God's church, whose fellowship we will enjoy in heaven. However, we cannot rejoice in what we consider to be a false spirit that is leading these people into teachings and practices that are not in accord with Scripture.

The "tongues" of Pentecost

It is now time to look into the New Testament to learn what comprised the genuine gift of speaking in tongues. We will compare what Scripture says about speaking in tongues with what is going on in the Pentecostal/charismatic movement today.

Saint Luke records the first episode of tongues-speaking. This occurred on Pentecost Day, the Jewish harvest festival celebration:

> All of them were filled with the Holy Spirit and began to speak in other tongues *[glossai]* as the Spirit enabled them. Now there were staying in Jerusalem God-fearing Jews from every nation under heaven. When they heard this sound, a crowd came together in bewilderment, because each one heard them speaking in his own language *[dialektos]*. Utterly amazed, they asked: "Are not all these men who are speaking Galileans? Then how is it that each of us hears them in his own native language *[dialektos]*? Parthians, Medes and Elamites; residents of Mesopotamia, Judea and Cappadocia, Pontus and Asia, Phrygia and Pamphylia, Egypt and the parts of Libya near Cyrene; visitors from Rome (both Jews and converts to Judaism); Cretans and Arabs—we hear them declaring the wonders of God in our own tongues *[glossai]*!" (Acts 2:4-11).

By miraculously enabling the disciples to speak in unlearned foreign languages on Pentecost Day, God was announcing that the Holy Spirit was being poured out upon the church as promised. Furthermore, this tongues-speaking episode made it clear that the gospel of Jesus Christ was meant for all people and should now go out into the whole world. It also made clear that this message was accompanied by the sanctifying power of the Holy Spirit.

In his account of Pentecost, Luke describes how Christ's disciples were filled with the Holy Spirit. As a result, they were capable of declaring the wonders of God to people of various nations in their own tongues, or languages (Acts 2:11), so that these foreign visitors could understand and profit from what was being said. By giving the list of people who were capable of understanding the disciples, Luke wanted to make it clear that the disciples spoke *real* languages. He explained that each one heard them speaking in his own language. The Holy Spirit had complete control of the disciples' tongues, enabling them to share the gospel of Christ with all who were present.

In bestowing the supernatural gift of tongues upon the disciples, the Spirit employed their faculty of speech to produce real languages, yet the words they spoke did not originate from within themselves. Rather, the words came from the Spirit himself. We do not know if the Spirit enabled each disciple to understand what he himself was saying. The point of emphasis is that the foreigners who were present felt at home in what they heard: "We hear them declaring the wonders of God in our own tongues [languages]!" (Acts 2:11).

In the above passage, the Greek word *dialektos* (from which the English word *dialect* is derived) is used interchangeably with *glossa*. *Dialektos* means "the language spoken by a particular nation or group of people." This is also the meaning of *glossa* in the verses above.

The word *glossa* (singular) as used in the New Testament can denote various things: the organ of speech (the tongue), the language spoken by the tongue, and the group that speaks a certain language. These three uses of *glossa* would indicate that the gift of the Spirit called speaking in tongues employed genuine languages that were used in everyday communication by groups or nations. The NIV, quoted throughout this book, regularly uses the word *tongues* to translate the Greek word *glossai* (plural), used by Luke in Acts 2 and by Paul in 1 Corinthians 12:10. But in each instance in a footnote the NIV gives the alternative translation "languages," an honest translation of the Greek word *glossai*. Wherever this word appears in the text to designate an extraordinary gift of the Spirit using the faculty of speech, the word *languages* could just as well appear in the English text.

Among the early church fathers, Saint Augustine regarded the tongues spoken on Pentecost as genuine languages confirming God's intention not to hide the gospel from the non-Jewish nations and peoples. He wrote: "These were signs adapted to the time. For there behooved to be that betokening of the Holy Spirit *in all tongues, to shew that the Gospel of God was to run through all tongues over the whole earth.* That thing was done for a betokening, and it passed away."[1]

Gentiles speak in tongues

On another occasion, the Holy Spirit gave the gift of speaking in tongues to the gentile Cornelius and his household. Luke tells us: "The circumcised believers who had come with Peter were astonished that the gift of the Holy Spirit had been poured out even on the Gentiles. For they heard them speaking in tongues *[glossai]* and praising God" (Acts 10:45,46). Peter had this to say about the episode: ". . . God gave them the same gift as he gave us, who believed in the Lord Jesus Christ" (Acts 11:17).

The same gift of speaking in tongues that had been given to Jewish disciples in Jerusalem on Pentecost Day was given to Cornelius and his gentile group. Those who heard them heard actual languages. It was, in a limited way, a repeat of the original Pentecost Day.

Tongues-speaking at Corinth

From what Paul wrote in 1 Corinthians, it is evident that the Holy Spirit gave the supernatural gift of speaking in tongues to other Christian congregations as well: "To each one the manifestation of the Spirit is given for the common good. To one there is given . . . to another speaking in different kinds of tongues, and to still another the interpretation of tongues" (12:7,8,10). Once again, the Greek word *glossai* is used to designate the miraculous speech bestowed by the Holy Spirit.

In connection with the use of tongues-speaking at Corinth, Paul introduces us to the gift of interpretation. He says that God gives "to still another the interpretation of tongues. . . . Do all speak in tongues? Do all interpret?" (1 Corinthians 12:10,30). Later Paul adds: "He who prophesies is greater than one who speaks in tongues, unless he interprets . . . For this reason anyone who speaks in a tongue should pray that he may interpret what he says. If anyone speaks in a tongue, . . . someone must interpret" (14:5,13,27). The gift of interpretation can be given to someone other than the tongues-speaker. Or the two gifts can be combined, for Paul advises: "Anyone who speaks in a tongue should pray that he may interpret what he says" (verse 13). In other words, the man should pray that his understanding, not just his faculty of speech, take part in the gift of speaking in tongues.

When a tongue is used in a congregational setting, interpretation must be present. The apostle goes so far as to command, "If there is no interpreter, the speaker should keep quiet in the church and speak to himself and God" (14:28).

Known languages or ecstatic speech?

In assessing whether the modern Pentecostal/charismatic tongues-speaking is in accord with Scripture, we must ask a very basic question: Were the tongues used by the Christians at Corinth different from those listed in the book of Acts? As we have seen, the Pentecostals and charismatics do not speak in foreign languages but in a kind of rhythmic speech composed of short syllables, which they call a praise language. They claim that their language may not parallel the known languages used in Acts but that it does parallel the speech used in Corinth.

There has been division on this issue from ancient times. Chrysostom and Augustine both said that the tongues spoken at Corinth were real languages. Chrysostom was quite insistent about it. On the other hand, Tertullian, an early Pentecostal who belonged to the Montanist sect, took the opposite position.

A well-known and highly respected Lutheran expositor of the New Testament, R. C. H. Lenski, takes the position that the "tongues" described in the New Testament are always known languages.

Robert Glenn Gromacki, a student of the tongues movement, also believes that whenever the word *glossa* ("tongues") appears in the Greek text, including in 1 Corinthians 12–14, it refers to a genuine language.[2]

However, even some conservative Bible commentators leave room for the possibility that the gift of tongues in 1 Corinthians could have been the ability to utter sounds that do not conform to any known language patterns.

Two possible scenarios at Corinth

Those who admit the possibility that the gift of tongues in 1 Corinthians could have been the ability to utter sounds that do not conform to any known language patterns are divided in their understanding of the source of the Pentecostal/charismatic gift of tongues. They construct two different scenarios. One group says that among the Corinthians some possessed the legitimate gift of tongues, but others were using a non-Christian ecstatic speech and passing it off as the true manifestation of the gift of tongues. This latter group is to have borrowed their "gift" from the heathen religions of the day.

Paul L. Maier holds this view. He concludes that the tongues at Corinth and those used on Pentecost Day were two different forms of glossolalia.[3] He categorizes the Corinthian tongues as an "irrational utterance"[4] and writes that many religious historians say the Corinthian Christians were deceiving themselves into thinking they had God's gift of tongues when in truth they had reverted to a form of religious ecstasy and glossolalia that was common in the Greco-Roman mystery cults.[5]

Is this scenario possible? There is no doubt that ecstatic speech was used in heathen religious practices. F. F. Bruce, in *Paul: Apostle of the Heart Set Free,* says that glossolalia, or tongues, was in itself not peculiar to Christianity. He points out that for a long time Greece had experienced the ecstatic speech of the Pythian prophetess at Delphi and the enthusiastic prayers of the followers of Dionysus.[6]

While it would not have been impossible that the Corinthian Christians had tapped into the devilish powers of heathen religions, we must ask, Where is the scriptural evidence that they did? Saint Paul never hints that such was the case. In 1 Corinthians 12–14 Paul always speaks about the gift of tongues as the genuine article. In chapter 14 Paul never hints that anyone in Corinth was using the religious language of the pagans. In fact, he equates his own gift of tongues with theirs: "I thank God that I speak in tongues more than all of you" (verse 18). We find it difficult to imagine Paul instructing the Corinthians to *interpret* their tongue if that tongue were of heathen origin. We conclude that the gift of tongues practiced by the Corinthians was a genuine gift of the Holy Spirit.

This leads us to the second scenario of what was happening in Corinth. In this scenario God had given the church two kinds of genuine spiritual gifts, both of which are referred to as tongues. According to this scenario, *tongues* can refer both to the gift the apostles received on Pentecost Day (the ability to speak in known languages) and to the "praise tongue" that the Corinthians and even Paul enjoyed (ecstatic speech).

This is the stand that most charismatics take, at least those who are willing to admit that almost no modern-day tongues-speaking is made up of known foreign languages.

They seek support for their gift from how Saint Paul allegedly used this gift. They refer to 1 Corinthians 14, where Paul says that his *spirit* was praying (verse 14) and that the Corinthians were using their gift to praise God with their *spirit* (verse 16). This possibility is also admitted by some confessional Lutheran scholars on the basis of some textual evidence that seems to indicate a shift in the nature of the gifts.

One gift of tongues

Is this scenario possible? We believe that primary consideration must be given to the very first recorded episode of tongues: that which occurred among the disciples on Pentecost Day. It must be Luke who decides what speaking in tongues is. In his historical account of the early church and the work of the apostles, Luke clearly describes the nature of the gift of tongues. It was the ability to speak in different languages previously unknown to the speaker. We believe the textual evidence would have to be stronger if we are to conclude that between Pentecost Day and when Paul wrote to the Corinthians, God gave the church another gift of tongues.

Some appeal to Paul's reference in 1 Corinthians 13:1, "If I speak in the tongues of men and of angels" to prove that there are two kinds of tongues and that the "praise language" tongue is actually the tongue of angels. Yet Paul never says that he can speak those languages or that they are available to him. In the entire three-chapter section where tongues are under consideration, Paul never refers to the gift of tongues as the tongue that angels speak.

Furthermore, in 1 Corinthians 14:7-12, Paul compares speaking in tongues to a trumpet sounding notes. In order to convey any meaning to the hearer, the trumpet must produce a pattern of sound, not just random noise. In a similar way, speaking in tongues must be interpreted if it is to spiritually build up the congregation. If it can be interpreted, it must be a known language and not a nebulous praise tongue composed of ecstatic speech and random syllables strung together. Even if we admitted that some type of interpretation of modern tongues might be possible, given their simple-syllable nature, any interpretation would be more like a revelation directly from God rather than an actual translation (even an interpretation) of what the tongues-speaker was saying.

It is clear from 1 Corinthians 14 that the gift of tongues had a place in the private prayer life of a person who had received the gift. Paul speaks about praying in his spirit while his mind was unfruitful. That is, he admitted to a certain spiritual benefit from speaking in an unknown language, even if his mind could not understand it (verse 14). Yet even so, Paul wanted to be able to understand what he was saying so that his mind was also edified. And when he was working with fellow Christians, he always wanted to pray and sing also with his mind so that his fellow Christians would be edified. How would he be able to do this? By interpreting the tongue he had been using (and this would entail the separate gift of interpretation). If Paul could interpret the tongue he had been using to praise God, then that tongue was a real language spoken by other people in a foreign country.

In this regard we should also note that at least one charismatic author makes much of the fact that Paul uses the word *interpret* instead of *translate* in 1 Corinthians 14:5,13. Consequently, he claims, Paul is not describing actual languages but, rather, ecstatic speech for which there would only be an "interpretation," or explanation.

This argument, however, is not supported by the Greek word Paul uses, which specifically means "to translate." In their exhaustive and scholarly work *A Greek-English Lexicon of the New Testament*, Bauer, Arndt, and Gingrich list "translation" as the first meaning of the word. They also point out that this is the same word used in the Greek version of Genesis 42:23: "They did not realize that Joseph could understand them, since he was using an *interpreter*," which, of course, refers to a translator. The genuine gift of tongues, therefore, is the miraculous ability to speak an unfamiliar or unlearned foreign language. The genuine gift of interpretation of tongues is the miraculous ability to understand and translate an otherwise unfamiliar foreign language.

We believe that Scripture indicates that the gift of tongues God gave the church at Corinth is the same gift God had given the church at Pentecost. Because at Pentecost there were people from all over the world present in Jerusalem who could understand those languages, it was appropriate for the disciples to speak them out loud. They were edifying the people to whom they were speaking, for the people themselves could understand the tongue. Paul's concern that tongues be used for edification had been met at that time—the church had been edified.

During the ensuing years, God continued to give the church this gift at certain times. The gift continued to show that the gospel was for the whole world. Those who had this gift used it for their personal edification, even when they did not understand the meaning of the words they spoke. In a church setting, however, where everyone spoke a common language, Paul said that the gift should be used for that purpose, that is, for private edification. But if there was someone present who could interpret it, then it could be spoken out loud and used to edify the church. Otherwise, the person with the gift should keep silent.

Does the modern tongues movement fit this picture?

The kind of tongues-speaking used today—a language made up of ecstatic, nonsensical sounds—simply cannot fit into Luke's description of the first tongues-speaking episodes in the church nor into 1 Corinthians 12–14, where Paul offers the church instructions regarding tongues-speaking. To summarize our position: We do not believe that there is any compelling textual evidence to suggest there were two distinct gifts of tongues given to the church by the Holy Spirit. The speaking of real languages under the Holy Spirit's influence is the single gift the Scriptures define as tongues. Therefore we conclude that the gift of tongues given to some in the church at Corinth was the original gift of speaking in foreign languages that was practiced at Pentecost and that the gift of tongues as practiced today is a counterfeit.

There is also a discrepancy between the purpose of tongues-speaking as practiced today and its purpose in Corinth. We have already seen that tongues-speakers use their gift primarily for what they consider personal edification, as a personal prayer language. Tongues-speakers admit that interpreting their brand of tongues (a simple-syllable language) is a very subjective matter, so in most cases, there is no real attempt to interpret them.

But this is far from what Paul was promoting. Paul was asking the Corinthians, particularly those who were using the true gift of tongues as a prayer language, "Is this what you really desire: prayer without understanding?" And then Paul clinched his point by revealing his personal determination: "What shall I do? I will pray with my spirit, but I will also pray with my mind; I will sing with my spirit, but I will also sing with my mind" (1 Corinthians 14:15). Paul says that he is determined to have the gift of interpretation when he prays and when he sings so that he prays and sings also with his mind. Otherwise, he will not pray or sing in a foreign language. For Paul the gift of tongues must be accompanied by the gift of interpretation (and thus also understanding), or he will not use it. He encourages the Corinthians: Either edify the assembly with your interpreted tongue, or keep still. And even when you use it privately, seek to interpret it so your mind will be fruitful. This fact shows that modern tongues are a counterfeit. They are basically untranslatable and unable to be used as a tool to edify the congregation, so of necessity they must be relegated to a private prayer language that is unable to edify the mind of the user.

Another evidence that the modern gift is a counterfeit is the place it plays in the average Pentecostal's faith. We have already read how the modern Pentecostal movement began. Charles Parham offered the challenge to his Bible college class to learn from Scripture what was the sign that a person had been born again. The class came back with the unanimous conclusion that speaking in tongues was that sign.

Consider what that meant for Christians in that church. Unless they spoke in tongues, they were not born again, or at least they were not baptized by the Holy Spirit. What a burden this placed on these people!

Is speaking in tongues a gift that every believer can expect to receive from the Holy Spirit? Paul writes, "To another [is given] speaking in different kinds of tongues" (1 Corinthians 12:10). The words "to another . . . different kinds of tongues" inform us that one person was gifted, if it pleased the Spirit, to speak several languages but that not everyone was gifted with that ability. Not everyone could expect to receive the gift. The Holy Spirit apportioned the gift of tongues as he saw fit.

Further on in chapter 12, Paul asks these rhetorical questions: "Are all apostles? . . . prophets? . . . teachers? Do all work miracles? . . . have gifts of healings? . . . speak in tongues? . . . interpret?" (verses 29,30). With these questions, Paul once more emphasizes the fact that the Holy Spirit does not give the same gifts to each believer. When, for example, the apostle asks, "Do all speak in tongues?" the answer is no!

Yet we continually read in Pentecostal/charismatic literature that *all* gifts are open to *all* believers of *all* time. This claim is patently false!

It is indeed sad to read accounts in Pentecostal/charismatic literature of Christians who have tarried (waited) for hours—even days, weeks, months, and years—in eager anticipation of the gift of tongues, because it is considered to be available to all.

It is true that today some charismatic churches tone down their insistence on the gift. But even so, its predominance as the premier gift of the Spirit is so strong that many without it feel they are second-class Christians. A true spiritual gift can be received only when the Spirit desires to give it. Therefore, any group that says every Christian should have this gift and then seeks to make it so must be dealing with something that can be generated by human volition. Anyone who has witnessed the charismatic spirit as it is passed from one person to another can readily see how this is true.

Tongues constituted a sign for unbelievers

Paul gave this further word of admonition concerning the gift of tongues to the Corinthian congregation: "Brothers, stop thinking like children. In regard to evil be infants, but in your thinking be adults. In the Law it is written: 'Through men of strange tongues and through the lips of foreigners I will speak to this people, but even then they will not listen to me,' says the Lord. Tongues, then, are a sign, not for believers but for unbelievers; prophecy, however, is for believers, not for unbelievers" (1 Corinthians 14:20-22).

God threatened the Jews of Isaiah's time by telling them that he would send foreigners, or strangers, against them. The Jews had refused to listen to God, who pleaded with them through their prophets; so he would speak to them in languages they would not understand, languages foreign to them. He would speak to them in words spoken by the cruel and oppressive Assyrians, thereby signaling judgment against the Jews. But even then they would not listen. The foreign tongues of the oppressor would not change their hearts.

In his letter to the Corinthians, Paul is pleading with the members of the congregation to be mature in their thinking and to strive to realize the consequences of using uninterpreted tongues in their church services. Uninterpreted tongues only serve as a sign to an unbeliever, not as a means of communicating God's love. They have a negative effect upon the unbeliever, producing an aversion in his mind toward the believers and what they are doing and teaching. The unbeliever feels at a loss, for he can't relate to what the believers are saying and doing. He concludes that he has no part in the proceedings. The tongues are a sign to him that something strange is going on, and he wants no part of it. Far from being jolted away from his unbelief, far from having his heart softened for the implanting of faith, the unbeliever feels alienated from the congregation.

Furthermore, the tongues constitute a sign of his alienation from God, yes, even a sign of divine judgment against him. They signify that God recognizes his unbelief and excludes him from his kingdom because of it. "When God speaks in such an unintelligible way, He exhibits Himself 'not as one that is opening His thoughts to the faithful, but as one who is shutting Himself up from those who don't believe.' So the hardened unbelievers, having rejected the clear and unmistakable preaching of the Cross, find themselves confirmed, and even justified, according to their opinion, by this phenomenon."[7]

The foreign languages that the unbelievers, in particular the Jewish unbelievers, heard on the lips of Christians reminded them of how God dealt with unbelieving Israel in the Old Testament. Should, then, the Christians at Corinth extol the gift of tongues so highly, considering that the tongues' purpose was not to bring hard-hearted unbelievers to faith and save them but to underscore their unbelief by signifying their alienation from God and their impending judgment? Let those who possessed the true gift of tongues use their gift in the manner and for the purpose God intended!

The modern tongues movement, particularly that part of it that uses tongues in public worship, are flying in the face of what Paul says here. Yet when a Christian group claims that people *must* have this gift in order to be sure they are filled with the Holy Spirit, public speaking in tongues cannot be stopped. It is another indication that the Pentecostal/charismatic gift of speaking in tongues does not originate with the Holy Spirit.

This same pattern continues in regard to healings and other miracles, which we will consider in the next chapter.

11

THE GIFT OF HEALING, POWER EVANGELISM, AND PROPHECY

We will now turn our attention to what Scripture has to say about the true gifts of healings (and performing miraculous signs) and whether the practice of performing these miracles in the Pentecostal/charismatic movement parallels Scripture.

We are not warned specifically against avoiding false tongues. But Scripture contains a number of warnings against the miracles of false prophets. The mere fact that a person performs miracles does not mean that he is sent from God. In Deuteronomy 13 the Lord warned the Israelites against false prophets who might entice them with their miracles. For example, in Exodus the Egyptian sorcerers reproduced Moses' miracles and kept Pharaoh from following God's word to let Israel leave Egypt (7:11,12). In New Testament times, Paul prophesied the coming of the Antichrist "in accordance with the work of Satan displayed in all kinds of counterfeit miracles, signs and wonders, and in every sort of evil that deceives those who are perishing" (2 Thessalonians 2:9,10). Furthermore, Christ warned the church that "false Christs and false prophets will appear and perform great signs and miracles to deceive even the elect—if that were possible" (Matthew 24:24). That the ability to perform healings and other miracles in Christ's name is not a sure sign of being filled with the Holy Spirit is shown by this warning from our Lord: "Many will say to me on that day, 'Lord, Lord, did we not prophesy *in your name, and in your name* drive out demons and perform many miracles?' Then I will tell them plainly, 'I never knew you. Away from me, you evildoers!'" (Matthew 7:22,23).

The mere fact that you cannot explain something, even if it really is of supernatural origin, does not necessarily mean that it is of God. In the light of Jesus' warnings concerning the miracles of false prophets, we should examine whether modern healings and miracles fit the pattern of Scripture.

We wish to emphasize three aspects of New Testament healing that will help us evaluate the modern healing movement. First, when Jesus or one of his apostles performed a miracle, it was always successful. Second, not even the apostles could heal everyone. Third, the purpose of healing in the early church was to bear witness to the truth of the Word.

The success rate of healing in the early church

Perhaps the most telling evidence that the spirit who produces miracles in the modern Pentecostal/charismatic movement is not the Holy Spirit is the lack of success. When an apostle told a leprous person to be clean, that person was cured. When an apostle said to a dead person, "Rise up!" the dead came alive. When an apostle announced to a sick person, "You are healed!" the sickness or disease was gone. When Peter and John commanded the crippled beggar to walk, "Instantly the man's feet and ankles became strong. He jumped to his feet and began to walk" (Acts 3:7,8). Certainly that pattern was true also for Jesus.

The healings Christ and his apostles performed never missed. Yet the same cannot be said of the "healings" performed by today's faith healers. Recall the discussion in Chapter 6. Faith healers do not even come close to a hundred percent in their attempts to heal. Anyone who has been around modern faith healers has seen many who came to them to be healed but went away sick or who seemed to be healed but soon had a relapse.

The miracles of today's miracle workers simply do not stack up in comparison with Jesus' miracles or those performed by the apostles. While the healings Jesus accomplished were undeniable, the same cannot be said of the "healings" of faith healers. Our Lord's enemies never attempted to discredit him by denying that he actually performed a miracle. That they couldn't do, for the miracles were very evident to all. Friend and foe alike admitted that they were supernatural. The foes of Christ did not attack the authenticity of his miracles but rather their source and their timing. Jesus was criticized for healing on the Sabbath, and he was accused of being in league with Satan (Mark 3:1-6,22-30).

Neither Jesus nor the apostles failed at a healing and then blamed it on the person's (or their own) lack of faith, as so many modern faith healers do. Healings were performed on believers and unbelievers alike.

The Lord certainly accepts the prayers of Pentecostal and charismatic Christians who pray for healing and then humbly leave the outcome to him. But the evidence shows that the healings performed by Pentecostals and charismatics today— healings that flow out of their spirit—do not come from the Holy Spirit. They do not follow the perfect pattern of miracles in Scripture. Therefore, they are counterfeit.

Even the apostles could not heal at will

To the Corinthians, Paul wrote: "To another [is given] gifts of healing by that one Spirit. And in the church God has appointed . . . also those having gifts of healing" (1 Corinthians 12:9,28). The Greek phrase literally should be translated, "gifts of healings." Note the plural, "healings." The plural indicates that each healing that takes place is a gift by itself. No one is given the gift to carry on a healing ministry in which he has the continuous power to heal everyone and anyone who comes to be healed. No one has the power to heal at will. The same can be said about the ability to perform miracles.

In the early church, the Holy Spirit guided the apostles and others in the matters of whom to heal and when to heal. He then endowed the healer in that particular instance with power to heal.

Not even the apostles had the power to heal everyone, nor the continual ability to heal. Consider Saint Paul. He performed many healings and miracles during his missionary journeys. On the way to Rome during his first imprisonment, while shipwrecked on the Island of Malta, Paul performed a miracle, shaking off, without ill effect, a viper that had fastened to his hand. Then he healed the father of Publius, the chief official of the island. After that, he healed the rest of the people on the island who were sick and who were brought to him (Acts 28:1-10).

Yet while Paul was in Rome, he wrote a letter to the Philippian church in which he told how Epaphroditus, whom the Philippians had sent to help him, became ill and almost died. Epaphroditus' illness became somewhat of a burden to the missionary and certainly was a serious concern. Why didn't Paul heal Epaphroditus, sparing his friend much suffering and sparing himself much anxiety? Why not, indeed! Through God's mercy, Epaphroditus' life was spared, but Paul claimed no credit for the healing. We are not informed of any miraculous intervention by the apostle. Epaphroditus' healing came from the Lord, when and how the Lord willed.

Paul was released from that imprisonment, but some years later was arrested again and found himself in Rome. During this second imprisonment, Paul wrote his final epistle, his second letter to Timothy. In it he explains that he left Trophimus sick in Miletus (2 Timothy 4:20). Though Paul needed Trophimus, he did not heal him. Nor did he heal Timothy's stomach ailment, which he mentions in this same epistle. Instead, he prescribed a home remedy, some wine. (Perhaps Paul had in mind that the acidity of the wine would counteract the alkalinity of the drinking water, which may have been causing Timothy's problems.)

Consider Paul himself, who was burdened with a "thorn in [the] flesh" (2 Corinthians 12:7). Three times he prayed, asking God to heal him. He was not healed. It was God's will for Paul to keep his thorn in the flesh. The working of miracles, including miracles of healings (as gifts of the Holy Spirit), had ceased for Paul.

Obviously, those who had the gifts of healings in the early church did not have the ability to heal everyone. Yet this is what many Pentecostal/charismatic healers claim for themselves.

There is absolutely no scriptural basis, no scriptural parallel, for the healing services sponsored by many charismatic and Pentecostal groups. They advertise and conduct so-called healing services with the claim "Come one, come all. We will heal you." In Chapter 6 we dealt extensively with faith healers and saw the fraud, deception, and scandals often connected to their activities.

What's wrong with power evangelism?

Charismatics point to Jesus' ministry. He displayed a twofold pattern wherever he went: proclamation and demonstration. First he preached repentance and the gospel. This was followed by casting out demons, healing the sick, and raising the dead, thus proving he is the anointed One who has brought the kingdom.[1]

What is wrong with wanting to imitate Jesus? Nothing—if the Lord wants his church to continue performing miracles as he did. Scripture does not support this, though. Even if it did, Pentecostals and charismatics would have a hard time equating Jesus' healing ministry with theirs. We have already demonstrated that the miracle-working powers of Pentecostals are far less than they claim. When Pentecostal/charismatic faith healers claim to be the Lord's agents to bring physical healing into the world, those faith healers had better be sure that their power is the same as that shown by Christ and the disciples. The power of Christ and his apostles acted immediately and was one hundred percent effective. Their power was combined with a humble desire to preach the death and resurrection of Christ, and on occasion they had to keep people from misinterpreting their ministry of healing. Even the best of the Pentecostal/charismatic community has trouble keeping that emphasis. In short, they promise more than Christ promises, and in their attempts to deliver on their promises, they come up short.

The facts speak for themselves. More often than not, the proponents of power evangelism fail in their attempts at the supernatural. Although they claim to have the Spirit's gift of prophecy or the ability to heal or to perform other miracles, they often fail. Failures are clear indication that the claimants do not possess the miraculous gifts of the Spirit. Far from lending proof to the gospel, they belie a cruel hoax, a charade on the part of the gospel messenger. Edward Gross points out, "The omnipotent and omniscient Lord cannot be the source behind a miracle manifesting weakness, incompleteness, or confusion."[2]

Healing in the early church testified to the power of Jesus and the truth of his Word

Healings, as well as other miracles performed by Christ, his apostles, and those upon whom the apostles laid their hands, were signs calling on people to believe in Christ. Our Lord told the Jews: "Believe the miracles, that you may know and understand that the Father is in me, and I in the Father" (John 10:38). "Believe me when I say that I am in the Father and the Father is in me; or at least believe on the evidence of the miracles themselves" (14:11). Nicodemus showed that his heart had been captured in part by the signs Jesus did, for he confessed to the Savior: "Rabbi, we know you are a teacher who has come from God. For no one could perform the miraculous signs you are doing if God were not with him" (3:2).

Recall the warning the writer of Hebrews gives: "We must pay more careful attention, therefore, to what we have heard, so that we do not drift away. How shall we escape if we ignore such a great salvation? This salvation, which was first announced by the Lord, was confirmed to us by those who heard him. God also testified to it by signs, wonders and various miracles, and gifts of the Holy Spirit distributed according to his will" (2:1,3,4).

Recall the time—soon after Pentecost—when Peter and John healed the crippled man. What explanation did they give for the healing? "By faith in the name of Jesus, this man whom you see and know was made strong. It is Jesus' name and the faith that comes through him that has given this complete healing to him, as you can all see" (Acts 3:16). Jesus, who was crucified and buried, whom the disciples had claimed to have seen alive but whom the enemy said was still dead, had wrought this miracle. The miracle simply underscored the fact that Jesus really was alive and in heaven and that he rules from there in power and glory. Peter had appealed to the Savior, saying, "In the name of Jesus Christ of Nazareth, walk" (verse 6). The healings, like the other miracles, were signs testifying to Jesus.

The words with which Saint Mark concludes his gospel come to mind: "The disciples went out and preached everywhere, and the Lord worked with them and confirmed his word by the signs that accompanied it" (16:20).

Most Pentecostal/charismatic healers profusely give glory to Jesus for any miracles they perform. However, the fact that they are not completely successful and that many of their miracles are shown to be temporary or incomplete flies in the face of Christ and his power. What a shame that so many flock to be healed in Jesus' name, only to find that Jesus' representative can only effect temporary or incomplete cures on only some of their diseases. Is Jesus' victory temporary or incomplete or intended only for some? Would Jesus want credit for this sort of healing ministry? Only a one hundred percent success rate, such as was present in the early church, adequately bears witness to Jesus' power and the truth of his Word.

Conclusion

We conclude that the healings and miracles of the modern Pentecostal and charismatic movements fall short of the pattern we find in Scripture. To many, especially to those yearning to be free from the ravages of sickness, the faith healers appear to be God's gift to us in these latter days. But when compared with the early church, it becomes clear that the modern healing movement lacks the success rate and a mature understanding of the nature of the gift of healings and miracles in the early church. It also gives an adverse witness to Jesus' power and complete victory over sin. It comes from a false spirit and can only be labeled a counterfeit.

We are not alone in our conclusions. Donald Hillis reminds us of three things we ought to consider when we evaluate the movement:

1) A high percentage of illness is self-induced. What is psychosomatically induced can often be psychosomatically destroyed. Christian Scientists and other sects and cults recognize the existence of this phenomenon and operate on the basis of it. By no stretch of the imagination can their activities be termed either scriptural or Christian, and yet they work healings. Psychosomatic healing has its place, but it is wrong to attribute divine character to it and to exploit it as "miracle healing."

2) Healings can be worked through the power of Satan, for Scripture clearly describes him as a miracle worker. Satan can bring on illness, disaster and death (as in the case of Job and his family). He can also take away illness. Jesus' warnings against false prophets who would work miracles, signs and wonders—as well as Paul's warning in Second Thessalonians—are cause enough to make us suspicious of the claims of the so-called faith healers of our day. Christians must take heed lest they follow the miracles of deceivers instead of the truth of Christ.

3) God heals. In the past he bestowed "gifts of healing" on individuals. But similar gifts of healing are not apparent today, for what are called gifts of healing simply do not match the gifts described in the Book of Acts. God still heals today, but he heals in answer to prayer, as we read in James 5.[3]

Prophecy in its narrow and broad sense

In Chapter 6 we examined the role prophecy plays in the Pentecostal/charismatic movement.

In 1 Corinthians, the apostle Paul writes glowingly concerning the gift of prophecy, recommending it as a gift that every believer ought to desire:

> Follow the way of love and eagerly desire spiritual gifts, especially the gift of prophecy. For anyone who speaks in a tongue does not speak to men but to God. Indeed, no one understands him; he utters mysteries with his spirit. But everyone who prophesies speaks to men for their strengthening, encouragement and comfort. He who speaks in a tongue edifies himself, but he who prophecies edifies the church. I would like every one of you to speak in tongues, but I would rather have you prophesy. He who prophesies is greater than one who speaks in tongues, unless he interprets, so that the church may be edified (14:1-5).

What is the gift of prophecy? Theologians have correctly divided prophecy into two categories, narrow and broad. In its narrow sense, prophecy is the result of direct revelation to an individual by the Holy Spirit; it includes foretelling future events.[4] In the scriptural sense of the term, a prophet does not mean a foreteller of future events, but a revealer of God's will to man; though the latter may (and sometimes does) include the former. So the gift of prophecy was that charism (gift) which enabled its possessors to utter, with the authority of inspiration, divine strains of warning, exhortation, encouragement, or rebuke and to teach and to enforce truths of Christianity with supernatural energy and effect.[5]

Paul and the apostles were prophets in this narrow sense of the word, receiving at times direct revelations from God, which they were authorized to communicate to others. Agabus, a prophet mentioned in Acts, did not speak words to the entire church of all ages, as the apostles did, but he also had the gift of prophecy in the narrow sense. He predicted a famine through direct revelation of the Lord (11:28).

Although Scripture does not make clear distinctions between the kinds of revelation this or that prophet received, it leads us to understand that prophets in the narrow sense of the term used their gift in a specialized way as the needs of the church dictated. However, Scripture also speaks of prophecy in a broader sense—a gift that served more for the general edification of the church. It was the ability to speak forth the wonderful truths of God as these have been revealed through the prophets and apostles by inspiration of the Holy

Spirit, with the result that souls were strengthened, encouraged, and comforted. The Holy Spirit used the intellect (as well as the personal faith) of the speaker and enabled him to speak forth the Word of Truth in an appropriate and timely manner. Prophesying, in the broad sense, since it speaks to people the wonderful apostolic message of salvation through Jesus Christ, edifies and strengthens Christians in their faith and also encourages them in holy living. The Holy Spirit accompanies the message with his grace, thereby making it his vehicle to accomplish his work in the minds and hearts of the hearers.

For example, Paul lists the gift of prophecy in Romans 12. There he is speaking of prophecy in the broad sense, as a gift used to edify the congregation. Note that it is included in a list of the more general gifts used in the ongoing work of the congregation, gifts associated with being witnesses and teachers of the gospel and serving one another in brotherly love. Paul says, "If a man's gift is prophesying, let him use it in proportion to his faith" (verse 6). The Greek word for *proportion* can mean "agreement" and also "right relationship." The personal pronoun "his" is not in the Greek text. The meaning is that whenever one prophesies, whatever it is that he tells God's people must be in agreement with the Christian faith that has been delivered to the saints (Jude 3). Everything that does not agree with this faith or doctrine is in error. Calling for this kind of "check and balance" to what is true prophecy and what is not distinguishes this gift from that of an apostle, whose inspired words were normative for the church, or even from the gift of Agabus, whose prediction of a future event was beyond question.

This same check and balance of a prophet's words is also found in Paul's instructions to the prophets at Corinth: "Two or three prophets should speak, and the others should weigh carefully what is said. And if a revelation comes to someone who is sitting down, the first speaker should stop" (1 Corinthians 14:29,30). While one person who was gifted with the ability to prophesy was speaking, another person with this gift might think of a pertinent truth that had been revealed by the apostles and that should then be injected into the present discussion. This prophet could then interrupt the first speaker, who was to be quiet and take his seat. The number of prophets prophesying at any one gathering was limited to two or three. Those who were gifted with the ability to prophesy were to carefully weigh what was being said. False teaching of any kind was to be recognized and subsequently corrected. "The spirits of prophets are subject to the control of prophets. For God is not a God of disorder but of peace" (verses 32,33).

These people were not speaking some new truth, nor were they speaking with the same authority as that of Jesus and his apostles. Their revelations were to be weighed carefully so that no false teaching might creep in. Sometimes the Lord would give a revelation to another prophet that would help explain the message of the first.

This kind of prophecy, prophecy in the broad sense, was no less spiritual, divine, or a product of the Holy Spirit's direction than prophecy in the narrow sense. It had an important place in the apostolic church.

When we deal with prophecy in the early church, we must keep it in the context of the early church and the special circumstances it faced. For quite a number of years, the New Testament church existed without the books that make up the New Testament portion of the Bible. They used the Old Testament, yet it needed to have the light of Christ's work shined on it so all could see how it was fulfilled in him.

It was quite a few years before God's people had the written words of the apostles, books they could read, meditate on, study, and use in their preaching and teaching. Gradually churches came to possess some of the inspired apostolic writings, but we must remember that the Holy Spirit was not finished with the New Testament until about 60 or 70 years after Pentecost. In this setting the church had a greater need for prophecy in the narrow sense that both directed the apostles what to write and at times gave the church other information it needed (2 Thessalonians 2:15).

Once the books of the New Testament began to be circulated among the churches, the need for special, direct revelations from God was no longer necessary. Church historians tell us that prophecy in the narrow sense passed from the scene, yet the gift of prophecy in the broad sense—preaching and teaching that drew from God's Word and applied it to the church—remained. Prophecy in the narrow sense followed the pattern of speaking in tongues and miraculous signs, which, in general, passed out of use once the church was established and the written Word was disseminated. While we cannot say that the Lord would never use someone to predict a future event, this kind of activity ceased at a very early stage in the church's history.

Those in the modern Pentecostal/charismatic movement claim that the gift of prophecy in the narrow sense never went out of existence, nor did God intend it to. Many charismatics claim to be the mouthpieces of God. Their messages are often subjective and difficult to interpret. Being subjective, they make it difficult to put Paul's check-and-balance system into effect.

If a person believes in direct revelation from God, how can he adhere any longer to the truth of the all-sufficiency of Scripture or to the principle of the infallibility of Scripture?

Do we recognize the awesome power that the possessor of "prophetic" messages wields over people's consciences to bind them with every "new" message that the prophet claims to have come from God? This is the very power that men like Oral Roberts have exerted over people's consciences in order to intimidate others into following them and contributing generously to their causes. The history of the tongues movement shows just how dangerous to the spiritual health of individuals and congregations the so-called gift of prophecy in the narrow sense can be. History also shows how easy it is to dupe even large groups of people with fraudulent, even ludicrous, prophetic utterances.

The Bible does not lead the church to expect any extrascriptural prophecy, but it does warn the church that false prophets will arise and impress people by their lies and lying wonders (Jeremiah 23:25,26,30-32).

The gift of prophecy in the broad sense is a precious gift all Christians would do well to desire and pray for. And may those who are blessed with this much needed gift use it in the church to instruct, exhort, admonish, strengthen, and encourage their fellow Christians and to bring about repentance and faith in unbelievers. As to the gift of prophecy in the narrow sense claimed by so many in the Pentecostal and charismatic movements, we consider it to be from a counterfeit spirit. It does not match the gift as God gave it to the early church.

12

THE GIFTS OF THE HOLY SPIRIT

The most precious gift God has given the Christian church is his Word. God's Word brings Christ to us, and through faith in him, we are made heirs of eternal life.

In addition to his Word, God has given the church spiritual gifts so that the Word can be spread and so that Christians can grow in faith and build each other up in love. The Holy Spirit began pouring out these gifts on the church on Pentecost Day, and he continues to pour them out to this day.

The subject of this book is not spiritual gifts but the Pentecostal/charismatic movement and its claim that God is again pouring out on his church particular gifts that have been unused since the time of the apostles. We have seen that this claim is false. Why? Not because the Lord has told us in his Word that he would stop giving these gifts. There is no passage that says that. Nor is our argument one from history, that is, that these gifts seem to have gone out of existence shortly after the death of the apostles. Our argument is simply this: what the Pentecostal/charismatic movement calls special gifts of the spirit—speaking in tongues, healing, miracles, and prophecy—does not fit the definition and pattern of these gifts in the early church. They are counterfeit.

We do not rule out the possibility that in the right circumstances God could again give these gifts to the church. And by refuting the claims of the Pentecostal/charismatic movement, we are not putting ourselves in the place of many liberal churches that deny the miraculous and have little place for these gifts.

We believe that God is performing miracles today on a daily basis in every aspect of our lives as Christians. We believe that God continues to heal in answer to our prayers and to the prayers others offer for us. We believe that God still gives the gift of prophecy to pastors, teachers, and others in the church so they can spread his Word accurately and with boldness. We believe that the gifts of speaking in tongues and interpretation have passed away, but we do not rule out the possibility that God could use these gifts for the good of his church if the conditions warrant it.

In order to balance the reactive nature of this book with a more positive statement, in this chapter we will look at other gifts the Lord has given his church, gifts that are not at the center of the debate with Pentecostals and charismatics. By looking at these gifts, we will see what a blessing spiritual gifts are to Christ's church and what a privilege we have to share in them.

Apostle

The gifts of the Holy Spirit include certain offices in the church, one of which is apostle. The term *apostle* was used both in a narrow sense (the Twelve) and in a broad sense, for others who helped the apostles. The word *apostle* literally means "messenger." When used in the broad sense, the term refers to men who assisted in bringing God's message of salvation to people. For example, Epaphroditus, Paul's "fellow worker and fellow soldier," was called the Philippian congregation's apostle, or "messenger" (Philippians 2:25). Barnabas, Andronicus and Junias, and James, the Lord's brother, were called apostles, all in the broad sense (Acts 14:14, Romans 16:7, Galatians 1:19). If the church today wanted to establish an office of apostle, it would have the right to so, but only in the broad sense. Perhaps the reason many churches have chosen not to use this term is because of the confusion it may cause.

In the narrow sense, *apostle* refers to the Twelve plus Paul. Paul writes, "In the church God has appointed first of all apostles" (1 Corinthians 12:28). Paul also testifies, "It was he who gave some to be apostles" (Ephesians 4:11). The qualifications for an apostle are stated in Acts 1:21,22: "It is necessary to choose one of the men *who have been with us the whole time the Lord Jesus went in and out among us,* beginning from John's baptism to the time when Jesus was taken up from us. For one of these must become *a witness with us of his resurrection.*" The teachings of the apostles form the foundation of Christ's church. Paul declares, "You are . . . built on the foundation of the apostles and prophets, with Christ Jesus himself as the chief cornerstone" (Ephesians 2:19,20).

Paul lists apostle as the foremost gift of the Holy Spirit to the church because, to the end of time, apostles remain the grand teachers in the church. First by their oral messages and now by their written word, they tell the story of God's saving grace through Christ. Their message is timely for every era. As the apostle Paul himself puts it, "Here is a trustworthy saying that deserves full acceptance: Christ Jesus came into the world to save sinners" (1 Timothy 1:15). Paul urged the Thessalonian Christians: "So then, brothers, stand firm and hold to the teachings we passed on to you whether by word of mouth or by letter" (2 Thessalonians 2:15). Whoever strays from the teachings of the apostles has either lost or is in danger of losing the precious gospel and the saving faith that comes through it.

The words of the apostles and prophets stand for all time as the Spirit's instrument to build and sustain his church. There is no other revelation given by the Holy Spirit that teaches us about Christ, brings us to faith, and guides us in holy living. Never can the apostles and prophets, as God's chosen and inspired vessels, be duplicated, enhanced, or replaced. The office of apostle, given to the Twelve and to Paul, is closed. If the gift of apostle is an ongoing benefit to the church from God, we would have to say that revelation is ongoing too, which, according to Scripture, is not the case. Once a house begins to be built on a foundation, there can be no more building the foundation. Because of this office, and because the office is closed, we can be sure that we have God's entire revelation and can be confident as we rest our faith in it.

In discussing the claims of the Pentecostals and charismatics, we did not touch on what they teach about the gift of apostle. They have no formal teaching about this, and many would accept the definitions we gave above. But we should note that some in the movement teach that the apostolic office continues to this day. Some even claim that there are apostles today equal to the original Twelve, equal also to Paul. One author writes:

> A major tenet of the Latter Rain movement during the 1950's was the idea that God never abolished the office of the apostle. [The] idea was circulated during the Latter Rain Movement that an all-conquering, overcoming end-time Church would not become visible until an elite band of end-time apostles emerged to lead her. [The] deceptions of the Latter Rain Movement did not die out in the 1950's. Most of the concepts taught in the Latter Rain churches have resurfaced in many contemporary charismatic congregations. The deception of elitism is alive in our [charismatic] congregations, still driving believers to search from church to church until they can identify that special group ordained by God for a higher purpose.[1]

Again, this is the extreme and not true of every Pentecostal or charismatic congregation. But in those churches that stress prophecy in the narrow sense, it is but a short step for someone to assume the role of apostle.

Prophet

Next to the gift of apostle is the gift of prophet: "In the church God has appointed . . . prophets" (1 Corinthians

12:28). "It was he who gave some to be . . . prophets" (Ephesians 4:11).

In the apostolic era, the church possessed prophets, whom we can define in the narrow sense as believers who received direct revelation from God intended for transmission to others. But these must have been few in number. There was Agabus, a prophet from Jerusalem who went to Paul at Antioch with a revelatory message from God, and also foretold the imprisonment of Paul (Acts 11:28; 21:10,11). Philip the evangelist had four daughters who had the gift of prophecy (21:8,9). However, their gift could have been that of prophecy in the general or broad sense. Anna, who welcomed the infant Christ in the temple, had the gift of prophecy (Luke 2:36-38). Judas and Silas are listed in Acts as prophets, who "said much to encourage and strengthen the brothers" (15:32). Luke does not state that they prophesied as the result of receiving direct revelations from God. Their message could have included direct revelation; however, Luke does not say one way or the other. In Acts 13:1 Luke reports that "in the church at Antioch there were prophets and teachers: Barnabas, Simeon called Niger, Lucius of Cyrene, Manaen . . . and Saul [Paul]." Somehow the Holy Spirit revealed to this group that Barnabas and Paul were to be set apart for his work. Perhaps the Spirit chose one of these qualified men to receive his prophetic message, which then was to be carried out by the whole group.

The New Testament does not give us many examples of this kind of prophetic activity, so it is hard to determine how common it was. Yet we are sure that the New Testament church from earliest times has had prophets, many of them. They are prophets in the broad sense of the term. They apply God's revealed Word to people in various situations and needs. One Bible commentator points out that all true preachers and teachers of the gospel are prophets in the general and broad sense, because they offer edification, admonition, and consolation to their hearers (1 Corinthians 14:3).[2]

Teacher

After prophets Paul lists teachers, those who have the ability to teach or instruct others in the Christian religion. "In the church God has appointed . . . teachers" (1 Corinthians 12:28). "It was he who gave some to be . . . teachers" (Ephesians 4:11). "We have different gifts, according to the grace given us. If a man's gift . . . is teaching, let him teach" (Romans 12:6,7).

The Spirit gives teachers knowledge, skill, and aptitude to do this work. To such believers the Holy Spirit also imparts the patience and zeal to spend great amounts of time studying the Scripture in order to know the truth, thus to be able to teach with authority and effectiveness.

Teachers help others comprehend and appreciate both the meaning and implications of Bible doctrine. Evangelists, pastors, and teachers (whether Christian school teachers, Christian college teachers, or seminary professors) are all of that teaching class and are precious gifts to the church. In our time we think also of Sunday school teachers, Bible class teachers, vacation Bible school teachers, and the like. They are all spiritual gifts to Christ's church. Whether they are guiding the learning of children or helping others delve into the gospel mysteries on a more profound level, without them none of us would have arrived at our present level of spiritual maturity.

Evangelist

In the apostolic era, the church had specially gifted people who were akin to our modern-day missionaries. They traveled to new places to win the hearts of people for Christ: "It was he who gave some to be . . . evangelists" (Ephesians 4:11). Philip was such an evangelist, as was Epaphras (Acts 8:5,12; Colossians 1:6-8).

Today, missionaries, or evangelists, preach the good tidings of salvation throughout the world, just as Christ prophesied they would (Matthew 24:14).

The ancient evangelists sometimes did miracles as signs confirming their gospel message (Acts 8:6). But whether the evangelists performed miracles or not, the Holy Spirit sanctified hearts through the message of the crucified and risen Christ. Jesus prayed to his Father in behalf of his disciples, whom he sent into the world: "Sanctify them by the truth; your word is truth. My prayer is not for them alone. I pray also for those who will believe in me *through their message*"

(John 17:17,20). Paul reminded the Thessalonian Christians that God called them "through our gospel, that you might share in the glory of our Lord Jesus Christ" (2 Thessalonians 2:14). Every evangelist of the Lord has full cause to be confident in the Holy Spirit's power of grace accompanying the true gospel of Christ whenever and wherever it is preached.

How grateful we are for this gift. In our recent or more distant past, we or our forefathers heard the gospel from the lips of some evangelist, and we are members of Christ's church because of the evangelist's willingness and ability to bring us the gospel.

Pastor

Paul lists another spiritual gift, the office of pastor (or shepherd). He writes, "It was he who gave some to be . . . pastors" (Ephesians 4:11). In ancient times pastors were the shepherds of the local flocks of believers. They remained when the apostles and evangelists moved on. Sometimes they served as contacts between the apostles and their own congregations. Pastors fed the flocks of Christ with the Word, which they were duty-bound to preach and teach. Paul wrote to Timothy, "Preach the Word; be prepared in season and out of season; correct, rebuke and encourage—with great patience and careful instruction" (2 Timothy 4:2). In New Testament times, since older men were generally chosen for this office, pastors were commonly called elders, which pointed to the dignity of the office (Acts 20:17). Other titles for a pastor in Bible times are bishop and overseer.

We are all familiar with this gift, and all of us have been blessed through it. God continues to call people into the office of pastor and gives them the ability to shepherd congregations with his Word.

Wisdom

Paul also lists the gift of wisdom: "To one there is given through the Spirit the message of wisdom" (1 Corinthians 12:8). Wisdom is good judgment in how to conduct the affairs of the church and to lead a Christian life. It is the true, trusted, and faithful application of God's Word in any given situation. This certainly includes the right application of law and gospel. Luke informs us that the enemy "could not stand up against his [Stephen's] wisdom or the Spirit by whom he spoke" (Acts 6:10). The use of this gift is illustrated by a church council member's prompt, godly advice or a pastor's skillful handling of a difficult congregational problem.

The believer with the message of wisdom knows how to address the need for salvation in others and to point them to the conduct that is appropriate for those who are saved. At the same time, godly wisdom enables him to set the proper example for others to follow. James writes: "Who is wise and understanding among you? Let him show it by his good life, by deeds done in the humility that comes from wisdom. . . . the wisdom that comes from heaven is first of all pure; then peace-loving, considerate, submissive, full of mercy and good fruit, impartial and sincere" (James 3:13,17).

What a blessing this gift is to our congregations. We have all benefited from those who are able to counsel and advise us with the wisdom God has given them.

Knowledge

Paul writes, "To another [is given] the message of knowledge by means of the same Spirit" (1 Corinthians 12:8). This is not mere human knowledge. Rather, it is knowledge that plumbs the depths of God's truth, his Holy Word. It is heartfelt knowledge of the details of the gospel, as well as the ability to convey this knowledge to others. True knowledge counters false teaching and helps Christians see through the errors Satan tries to introduce into the church.

Who of us has not benefited by the special gift of knowledge that God has given one or another of our Christian teachers? They may have inspired us to learn more about Christ or opened to us new vistas of understanding and insight.

As a side point, we might note what some in the charismatic movement understand this gift to be. John Wimber, in his book *Power Evangelism,* claims that this gift is the knowledge of what is going on in the life and even in the mind of the other person so that the Christian blessed with this gift knows what hidden sins to deal with or what personal problems to address.[3] Others in the movement claim it is the supernatural knowledge given to faith healers to enable them to identify people's ailments so as to work miraculous cures.

Faith

Paul writes, "To another [is given] faith by the same Spirit" (1 Corinthians 12:9). This is not saving faith, for all Christians have that. Rather, it is a particularly strong faith in God's power and grace. It is a faith that blossoms in times of great trials, stress, and hardships. It is a faith that does not doubt or waver but simply believes and relies upon the promises of God. This faith prays when it is difficult to pray and places matters in God's hands when it would be easy to give up on him. Heroic faith is willing to bear persecution, trusting that God has prepared something better than this present life for his believers.

An example of this faith is found in the hospital patient who calmly faces high risk surgery, or even death, with Paul's attitude: "I consider that our present sufferings are not worth comparing with the glory that will be revealed in us" (Romans 8:18). There is no shortcut to this faith. It comes from patient, diligent, prayerful study of God's Word and is cultivated by the Holy Spirit in the believer during times of testing (Romans 5:3-5; 1 Peter 1:6,7).

Such a faith is indeed a precious, even priceless, gift of the Holy Spirit. Who of us has not been inspired by people with this kind of faith? Their 20/20 spiritual vision into God's gracious care for them leads us to greater confidence in God's ability and willingness to help us.

Distinguishing between spirits

Paul writes, "To another [is given the gift of] distinguishing between spirits" (1 Corinthians 12:10). The apostle John exhorts, "Dear friends, do not believe every spirit, but test the spirits to see whether they are from God, because many false prophets have gone out into the world" (1 John 4:1). All Christians are to be on guard against false teachers and false doctrine. Distinguishing between spirits, however, refers to a special ability that goes beyond ordinary Christian watchfulness. This gift enables the Christian to distinguish between true and false prophets, thereby giving him the capability to warn the church against those who are false and to admonish the church to heed those who are true.

The gift of distinguishing between spirits includes, of necessity, the ability to distinguish between true and false teachings or doctrines. To test the spirits, one would have to possess a thorough knowledge of God's Word, especially of the doctrine of eternal salvation. Instead of accepting a prophet's teaching at face value, the Christian who is gifted with discernment is quick to test with Scripture whatever he reads or hears.

It should be noted that only true prophets can distinguish between spirits and thereby discern true and false teachings. The one who *teaches* falsehood has himself failed in discernment. Those who *follow* false prophets and teachers don't have the gift of discernment either. As the end of all things approaches, many will show a lack of discernment, for they will follow false prophets, eager to hear what they have to say, and in the process they will turn away from God's truth. Paul warns: "The time will come when men will not put up with sound doctrine. Instead, to suit their own desires, they will gather around them a great number of teachers to say what their itching ears want to hear. They will turn their ears away from the truth and turn aside to myths" (2 Timothy 4:3,4).

As we come closer to the end of time, love for the truth will diminish, while false doctrines and their teachers will multiply and flourish. Therefore, in the end time, the gift of discernment will take on ever greater importance yet will be in ever shorter supply. The gift of discernment is very much needed in the church today, when it is popular to go with the flow—to accept as truth whatever is popular at the moment or is recognized by the majority as acceptable. Many in the church will retreat from the truth and cling to error, especially when the error is couched in what appears to be supernatural works. However, this will not be the case with those who possess the gift of discernment nor with those who are wise enough to listen to them.

We are truly blessed to walk in the footsteps of a man like Martin Luther, who truly had the gift of distinguishing between spirits. He was not afraid to say to the false teachers of his day, "You are of another spirit." By God's grace he followed the teachings of Scripture and allowed the true Spirit of God to have his say in the church.

Among charismatics and Pentecostals, the gift of distinguishing between spirits appears to have been placed on the back burner. In its overwhelming zeal for ecumenism, the charismatic movement has been willing to compromise with false doctrine and to join in fellowship gladly with those who disseminate it. Many in the movement join hands with churches that deny some of the basic truths of how to gain eternal life.

Helping and serving others

Paul writes, "In the church God has appointed . . . those able to help others" (1 Corinthians 12:28). "If it [a man's gift] is serving, let him serve" (Romans 12:7). Those who possess this gift from the Holy Spirit are blessed with the ability, the work ethic, the humility, the love, the dedication, and the personal focus to take on tasks that benefit others. Those who have this gift see a task that needs to be done, know their own ability to accomplish it, and are willing to be involved, even if it requires sacrifice on their part.

Serving is the act of filling a need, whether that need is great or small. It is service for service's sake. It is looking for opportunities to help out, with no expectation of reward. Together with their acts of service, servers or helpers often provide much needed practical help. The seven deacons in the Jerusalem congregation were gifted to perform acts of service (Acts 6:1-7).

There are those in the congregation who feel uncomfortable in any role but service. They may not accept an office in the church; they may not attend congregational meetings; they may not want to serve on the evangelism committee ("Pastor, I just can't go out and talk religion to other people"). But they are the first to volunteer to serve and the first to be there when help is needed. They mow, paint, clean, bake, console the sick, deliver sustenance to the needy, and take on any number of other tasks, menial though they may be. They put their hearts into their work and do it well. They are people who possess a gift that is greatly needed by the church but not always given the appreciation it deserves. Often we don't notice their work, but we always benefit from it.

Administration

To some believers the Holy Spirit gives skills in managing and leadership: "In the church God has appointed . . . those with gifts of administration" (1 Corinthians 12:28). "If it [a man's gift] is leadership, let him govern diligently" (Romans 12:8). The gifts of administration include knowing what needs to be done and how to do it and having the skill and tact to direct others to help get the job done smoothly, efficiently, and promptly. Those who have this gift accomplish their work without fanfare and without stirring up resentment or causing conflict. These gifts of management can be combined with other gifts. A pastor or teacher, for example, may also be a good manager. Others who are blessed with this gift serve as church elders, trustees, chairpersons, or members of a committee or board.

Every congregational member receives the benefit of this spiritual gift.

Encouragement

Paul writes, "If it [a man's gift] is encouraging, let him encourage" (Romans 12:8). This gift promotes the fruit of good works in those who are justified by faith, showing them from the Scripture the right things to do or the proper course to take. It can also serve those who are suffering, thus affording them encouragement to remain strong in the faith and to remain steadfast at all times, even in times of persecution. This gift enables Christians who possess it to hold up the truth before God's people and urge them to be faithful to it. The gift of encouraging others, by its very nature, encompasses teaching, admonishing, guiding, and comforting. Encouraging others is one of the blessings that comes from the gift of prophecy: "Everyone who prophesies speaks to men for their strengthening, encouragement and comfort" (1 Corinthians 14:3). Of course, all encouragement must be based upon and in harmony with Holy Scripture (2 Timothy 4:2; Titus 1:9).

All Christians know people in their congregation who have an encouraging word from the Lord. What a blessing they are!

Contributing

Paul writes, "If it [a man's gift] is contributing to the needs of others, let him give generously" (Romans 12:8). People with this gift have a deep sense of compassion that makes the sufferings and needs of others their own concern. These people reach into their pocketbooks or pantries to provide for others. A believer who has this gift should use it with generosity. We would have to conclude that the gifts of helping, contributing, and showing mercy are related and are rooted in a deep love for other people, a love that is not content simply to talk but must act.

All of us benefit from the financial and material contributions of those who have this gift. In fact, they often make up for what others are unable or unwilling to give.

Showing mercy

Paul writes, "If it [a man's gift] is showing mercy, let him do it cheerfully" (Romans 12:8). This is the gift that moves a person to show loving-kindness to those in distress. This is another of those gifts that leads love into action. We could also refer to it as demonstrated sympathy or compassion. Those with this gift should never give the impression that they are making a sacrifice but should help the unfortunate or hurting in a cheerful way, counting it a privilege to ease another person's burden with a heartfelt gift of love.

Neither this gift nor most of the other gifts Paul lists in Romans 12 are what we might call spectacular. Yet every one of these gifts is vital to the spiritual life and general welfare of the congregation. To have a fellow Christian show us mercy when we are in need conveys to us the power of Christ's love in a unique way.

Other gifts?

Are there any other gifts of the Spirit, gifts not mentioned in Scripture, or are these the only ones? The church does not agree on this question. Personally, we believe that whenever additional gifts are needed in the church (for example, the wide range of musical abilities we need in our churches), the Holy Spirit supplies them. If a gift is no longer needed, the Spirit can withdraw it. The church needs the grace to recognize spiritual endowments in its people and the determination to put these gifts to good use to the glory of God and the benefit of all.

Have spiritual gifts been missing in the church?

One gets the impression from Pentecostals and charismatics that they have rediscovered spiritual gifts and their importance to the church. Perhaps they came out of congregations that lacked the gospel and therefore lacked the Spirit and his gifts.

Personally, we are continually thrilled at the power of the Spirit shown in the wisdom, knowledge, and leadership displayed in Christ's church over the ages. We see prophetic speech, sacrificial giving, and countless acts of mercy. We see people spreading the gospel and teaching God's truth to others. We witness patient and courageous reaction to suffering, brotherly and sisterly love, the willingness to serve others, and the ability to express faith in many ways.

How else would mission fields have been explored, established, staffed, and funded? How else would religious institutions of caring have existed? What other than the Spirit's power kept and still keeps martyrs faithful unto death? What brought about the Reformation of the church in the 16th century? What has led mothers and fathers to work and sacrifice to put their sons and daughters through years of schooling to become pastors and teachers? What has led many to witness their faith in Jesus Christ to neighbors, fellow workers, and friends? What drives men and women to build and staff schools and churches for teaching and preaching God's Word and to sacrifice greatly to do so? And don't forget the wonderfully gifted musicians and writers who have brought spiritual inspiration and comfort to countless believers by their work. The simple fact is that the church has always been blessed by its members owning and using spiritual gifts bestowed by the Spirit.

We should be constantly challenged to seek more gifts from the Holy Spirit and with his help to put them to good use. "Each one should use whatever gift he has received to serve others, faithfully administering God's grace in its various forms. If anyone speaks, he should do it as one speaking the very words of God. If anyone serves, he should do it with the strength God provides, so that in all things God may be praised through Jesus Christ" (1 Peter 4:10,11).

13

DRAWING POWER AND DOCTRINAL ERRORS

Why is the Pentecostal/charismatic movement so attractive? Why is it growing at such a fast pace?

Both the old and new segments of Pentecostalism agree that the Holy Spirit baptism they teach is the Spirit's way of revitalizing a dying Christianity. This is a key to understanding, at least in part, Pentecostalism's popularity in our time. Many professing Christians become involved in the movement because they believe their own spiritual lives have been lacking, and they want more out of their religion than they have been getting. Or they may have come to the conclusion reached by Charles Parham of Topeka, that the church as it presently exists lacks the vitality and the ability to carry out Christ's command to evangelize the world.

Many tongues-speakers are members of churches that have been bathed in liberalism and neo-orthodoxy. These are churches that emphasize the ecumenism of the World Council of Churches but neglect the message of the cross.[1]

Father Dennis Bennett is an example of one who endured a liberal theological background and later came to seek the "baptism." The priest had come into the Episcopal church two years after graduating from a theological school where extreme liberal humanism reigned. He received his education at the University of Chicago and Chicago Theological Seminary. The professor who taught the psychology of religion course was an avowed atheist. Agnosticism, skepticism, and humanism carried the day. The supernatural events reported in Holy Scripture were discounted. After 16 years in the ministry, Bennett felt "dry and hungry deep inside," having lost, as he expressed it, the "personal awareness of God" in his life.[2] Seeing the spiritual vitality that appeared to exist in a young charismatic couple, Bennett eventually came to seek for himself their baptism in the Spirit and speaking in tongues.

Wayne E. Oates suggests that where glossolalia breaks out, the church should take a close look at its own superficiality to see whether it is really dealing with the spiritual problems of its people.[3] A church that expounds Holy Scripture as the true, inspired Word of God and rightly applies the gospel to its people has a way of successfully dealing with its problems.

However, many Christians who go to their churches on Sunday morning spiritually hungering for God's Word come away starving, having been fed nothing but liberalism, humanism, and the social gospel.

Instead of faithfulness to God's Word (2 Timothy 3:14–4:2), many pulpits today promote modernism and neo-orthodoxy. Modernism teaches that all religious doctrines and practices must be accepted on the basis of whether they can fulfill people's needs. It teaches that religious and spiritual concepts are evolutionary and that no religion, including Christianity, can claim a monopoly on the complete truth. Modernism teaches that the Bible is not the sole authority in matters of faith and life. It teaches that all religions are good; its gospel is the social gospel.

In modernism man's own experiences become the standard of his religious values. The goal of all religious experience is a fully developed personality. Sin is merely a barrier to this development, not something that condemns. The fully integrated personality is best developed in a social environment that is patterned after the spirit of Jesus.

Under this system of thinking, sermons become mere moral lectures. Christ's perfect life and death are presented merely as examples of social idealism, not as the vicarious sacrifice of atonement for sins.[4]

Neo-orthodoxy is an attempt to push the pendulum of modernism back the other way. It is the theology of Karl Barth and Emil Brunner. Whereas modernism does not take sin seriously, this theology does. Man needs God's grace to change for the better. While modernism gives man a watered-down version of God—his only attributes being love and patience—neo-orthodoxy pictures him also as a God of judgment. Yet neo-orthodoxy takes a broad theological stance and believes that doctrinal formulation stymies theology. Neo-orthodoxy accepts the principles of higher criticism, which, in the final analysis, deny divine inspiration of the Bible and allow for errors in Scripture. It too denies the absolute authority of the Bible in matters of doctrine and practice. It teaches that the gospel message itself, not the Bible that contains it, is inspired. Thus the language of Scripture becomes largely symbolic.[5]

These theological positions, which have infiltrated thousands of churches, burden the church with a spiritual deadness and coldness. Many within the Pentecostal/charismatic movement have come out of such churches. And they consider their baptism in the Spirit and speaking in tongues as the means to salvage a dying church.

Looking for a show of strength

The Pentecostal/charismatic movement attracts many with the promise that Spirit baptism will equip and free them for service to the Lord. Stephen Clark, in *Baptized in the Spirit,* testifies that through his own experience of working to convert people, he became convinced that "some kind of power was needed." To him the "life in the Spirit" offered through the charismatic renewal was the answer. He flatly states that "life in the Spirit" is possible only to those who have received Holy Spirit baptism.[6]

Evangelist Oral Roberts is a prime example of a Pentecostal (now a Methodist who bears the charismatic label) who boldly laid claim to a ministry with the power to heal physical illnesses and impairments. After 12 years as a pastor in the Pentecostal Holiness Church, Roberts was ready to leave the ministry, a ministry he felt had become invalid and unable to meet the needs of the people.[7]

Roberts came to the conclusion that there is a difference between a Christian and a follower of Christ. A follower of Christ, or a disciple, is one who does what Jesus did, or tries to repeat the acts of Jesus, that is, perform miracles.[8] In his autobiography Roberts tells how he concluded that he would either have a ministry like Jesus' or get out of the ministry altogether. After a great deal of prayer, in which he laid out a test for the Lord, Roberts embarked on a healing ministry that made history. The prospect of physical healing has, without doubt, attracted many people to Pentecostalism. As soon as Roberts began his healing ministry, attendance at his services increased by leaps and bounds. He was offering more than eternal salvation; he was offering a solution to the immediate and vexing problems of bodily illness and infirmity.

Searching for something more

The classical Pentecostal movement seems to have arisen spontaneously in a number of places in America and around the world among those who wanted something more than they were getting from their churches. Many people join the Pentecostal/charismatic movement to know God experientially—in a more fulfilling way than just through doctrine.[9] The experience of speaking in tongues seems to offer the remedy for this void in their religious experience. This still remains a powerful motive for people to join the tongues movement.

In *Bread of Life,* Pastor Don Matzat (at the time, a leading Lutheran charismatic—he has since left the movement) contended that the experience of baptism in the Spirit is happening today just as it did on Pentecost and in 1900, and he pointed out, "It is taking place out of hunger, out of frustration, out of disenchantment with their religious experience: a merely doctrinal faith as opposed to an experiential knowledge."[10]

Longing for acceptance

There is a good reason to believe that many people who experience speaking in tongues do so not because they are led to it by studying Holy Scripture and its reference to tongues but because they trust the judgment of their friends and are persuaded by the sincerity and joyfulness of others. They want to share in the joyful experience.

The power of these two elements working together is the reason for the movement's popularity. A hunger for something to satisfy a spiritual void coupled with the witness of people who have found something that can produce spiritual euphoria accompanied by some pretty dynamic signs—these two elements combine to produce Pentecostalism's appeal.

Undermining justification by faith: the heart of the Christian faith

Evangelizing the world with the message of salvation through Jesus Christ is now a top priority in the Pentecostal/charismatic movement. However, in some of its teachings and practices—which we have had occasion to discuss at some great length—we find that it, in fact, compromises and even destroys the very gospel it proposes to take to the entire world.

We feel that many within the tongues movement would quickly deny that this is so. They want to hold on to forgiveness of sins through the blood of Christ. Yet they do not realize the serious implications of some of the statements they make, some of the attitudes they foster, and some of the practices and activities in which they participate. When we closely examine the tongues movement, we can only conclude that the central doctrine of Scripture, justification by God's grace through faith in Christ, and the integrity of Scripture are being challenged and compromised. We will look at why the central doctrine of Scripture, justification by faith in Christ, cannot be upheld in the movement.

The teaching of justification for all by the blood of Christ is the gospel message. By faith we are justified and made heirs of eternal life. Scripture abounds with the comforting, saving message that God justifies sinners for Jesus Christ's sake—thus declaring them not guilty of their sins. Instead of charging their sins to their account, God imputes to them the righteousness of Christ, which he earned for all sinners by his atoning sacrifice on the cross. This justification, this forgiveness of sins, this declaration of being righteous before God, comes to us sinners through personal trust in Jesus. No one's good works can save him, for every sin merits damnation from God. Saving faith trusts in God's grace alone, which is based on the sacrifice of Christ in behalf of a world of sinners. Possessing saving faith in Jesus Christ, the sinner trusts fully and completely in him alone for salvation.

The works Christians do are not the *cause* but rather the *result* of salvation, for they flow freely from faith as thank offerings to God. The whole matter of forgiveness of sins and salvation by God's grace through faith is summarized in a clear and concise manner by the apostle Paul:

> Now a righteousness from God, apart from law, has been made known, to which the Law and the Prophets testify. This righteousness from God comes through faith in Jesus Christ to all who believe. There is no difference, for all have sinned and fall short of the glory of God, and are justified freely by his grace through the redemption that came by Christ Jesus. . . . we maintain that a man is justified by faith apart from observing the law (Romans 3:21-24,28).

Paul gives this warning to all who would trust their good works to save them: "You who are trying to be justified by law have been alienated from Christ; you have fallen away from grace" (Galatians 5:4,5).

Do the Pentecostals and charismatics believe this? Most would say yes, certainly. But when we study the movement, particularly the charismatic side, it becomes clear that the spirit behind their spirit baptism and other signs and wonders is more important than the teaching of salvation by faith in Christ alone.

The charismatic's Roman Catholic connection

Earlier in this book we demonstrated at length that Protestant charismatics desire to carry on religious fellowship with their Catholic counterparts. The basis for this fellowship is not unity of doctrine, or even of faith, but, rather, their spirit baptism experience. For the average Catholic, taking part in the charismatic movement has not dampened his enthusiasm for Rome and its teachings and traditions. The charismatic experience actually grounds the Catholic more firmly in the delusion that the Church of Rome is the true church and that all the doctrines, all the customs, all the traditions, all the church and worship practices that are sponsored by the "true" church are appropriate—whether in harmony with Scripture or not.

When Protestant Christians see Holy Spirit baptism (often accompanied by speaking in tongues) among Catholic charismatics, they are convinced that these charismatics really have been filled with the Holy Spirit.

But can this be true? Consider the gospel of the Church of Rome. To a great extent it is a false gospel of work-righteousness. The Roman Catholic Church has many ways of denying justification by God's grace through faith and of substituting good works as the way to salvation. Roman Catholicism compromises the gospel by distinguishing between venial and mortal sins and then by laying down conditions for how those sins can be taken away. Rome compromises the gospel by teaching the doctrine of purgatory, a mythical place of punishment where one must go to pay the temporal punishment of his sins. This teaching implies that Jesus' death on the cross didn't redeem sinners from all sin. Rome also actively teaches about indulgences, which can be bought or obtained by doing good works. It teaches that its members can make sacrifices in this life so that their time in purgatory can be shortened. It teaches that its members should pray to Mary and the saints and rely on their "surplus of merit"—all of which is work-righteousness.

Perhaps the most blasphemous part of Rome's doctrine of work-righteousness is the Mass. Roman Catholicism teaches that the one sacrifice of Christ on the cross was not sufficient for all time; rather, it must be performed over and over by the clergy. Through the consecration of the bread and wine in the Mass, Rome continually "offers" Christ anew on its altars in unbloody sacrifices for the sins of the living and the dead. The precious gospel of Jesus Christ and his role in our lives is further compromised in the elevation of Mary to the status of a goddess who is supposed to intercede for believers.

All these teachings compromise and weaken the scriptural teaching of justification by God's grace through faith in Christ. In the words of Professor David Kuske, "Almost all of the teachings which have been added to the Bible in Roman Catholicism in some way or other deny Christ's full and free redemption."

By fellowshiping with the Catholic charismatic renewal, Protestant charismatics share in Catholic teachings and practices. Though they may personally believe the truth of justification by God's grace through faith in Christ alone, they nevertheless give the impression that Rome's teaching is an acceptable one. The trumpet thus sounds an uncertain note. What the world needs more than anything else is a crystal clear, unwavering, unyielding, uncompromising, robust presentation of the central truth of Scripture: man is justified by faith in Christ without the deeds of the law. "By grace alone, by faith alone, by Scripture alone" should be emblazoned on the church's banner as Christians everywhere go out to rescue sinners with the true and powerful message of salvation in Jesus Christ.

When Protestant charismatics join hands with Roman Catholic charismatics, they are doing just the opposite. They are giving a false witness to the gospel they claim to believe. In the process they show that their spirit is more concerned about maintaining itself and its powers than about bearing witness to the gospel of Christ.

Faith in Christ does not guarantee physical healing

In a previous chapter we saw that the Pentecostal/charismatic healing phenomenon does not fit with how the gift of healing was practiced in the early church. Even Pentecostals realize that their healing success rate falls far short of the apostles'. Over the years they have developed a number of explanations for why this is so. When we hear these reasons, we soon realize that all of them undermine justification by faith.

Remember, a basic Pentecostal/charismatic truth is that God wants to heal all diseases and that the work of Christ on the cross has enabled all to be healed. This statement makes it necessary to explain why some are not healed. The reason most often given is a lack of faith either on the part of the healer or on the part of the person who cannot be healed. But since the faith healer has already healed some people on any given day, his faith must be strong enough. So most often the problem is with the faith of the person who is not healed. Some have been known to claim that the sickness is God's punishment for sin and therefore cannot be healed or that Satan is behind the sickness. All these reasons compromise the gospel of Christ and attack the individual's faith in the Savior.

It is grossly unfair and dangerous to a person's faith and salvation to judge his spirituality—the strength or weakness of his faith—by the condition of his physical health. Many true Christians who are blessed with a strong faith suffer from bodily afflictions until the day they die. This was true of the apostle Paul and, no doubt, of Timothy also.

When a faith healer claims that if a person's faith is strong enough, he will be healed, that person may begin to harbor dangerous doubts if a healing does not take place. What if he is not healed, even though he felt at the time that he prayed with earnestness and sincerity of faith? What if some who have the same disease or the same physical impairment are healed and others are not? Does this sound anything like Paul's ministry or Christ's ministry?

Oral Roberts admits that he has failed many times to heal people. He has pointed out that two people with the same affliction could be in the same prayer line. One would be healed and the other not. Roberts said that only God knows what is inside us and what it really takes to bring out a miracle. For a miracle of healing to occur, Roberts looks to the faith of the person who desires healing.[11]

What about those many hopeful Christians who aren't healed, even though they have been assured God wants them well, and who have been told that it's their own lack of faith that's responsible for their failure to be healed? How many Christians have had their weak and fragile faith weakened even more and even destroyed because their hope of healing was not met with a miracle? Only judgment day will reveal it.

Pastor Don Matzat tells of visiting an elderly lady in the hospital who was on the verge of death. As she clasped his hand, she began to cry. Her words to him were truly pathetic: "I am so sorry, Pastor. . . . I am so sorry that I do not have the faith to be healed." Fifteen minutes later she died. Why this confession of guilt? Two well-meaning women had visited her earlier and informed her that if she had the faith for it, she would be healed. What an intolerable burden they laid on her conscience as she lay dying.[12]

Scripture gives no cut-and-dried description of the relation of faith to healing. Interestingly, many of the healings reported in the New Testament benefited people who had not yet been brought to faith in Christ. Christ healed all who appealed to him.

Never, ever, should a person's justifying faith in Christ be judged by the state of his health or by whether he is healed in answer to prayer. The faith that saves, that justifies, the sinner is childlike trust in the suffering, death, and resurrection of Jesus Christ in behalf of a world of sinners. This faith saves, even in moments of weakness—which every Christian experiences. Justification by faith is in serious danger whenever anything less is taught.

The relation of faith to physical healing

Let's carry our present discussion a step farther.

Many charismatics today equate atonement for sin with healing of physical ailments. One charismatic author writes: "In essence, as we have seen, physical healing is of one piece with such things as forgiveness, or the final conquest of death. Therefore we should lay hands on the sick and pray for them to be healed, with the same certainty that we proclaim the forgiveness of sins or preach the resurrection."[13]

What is the relation of Christ's work to the physical illnesses, diseases, and deformities we experience in life? Scripture gives us an answer, and as we discover that answer, we will see how diabolical the Pentecostal/charismatic claim concerning healing is.

We find our answer in Isaiah 53:4,5: "Surely he took up our infirmities and carried our sorrows, yet we considered him stricken by God, smitten by him, and afflicted. But he was pierced for our transgressions, he was crushed for our iniquities; the punishment that brought us peace was upon him, and by his wounds we are healed."

Commenting on the first clause in the quotation above, August Pieper, a highly respected Lutheran theologian, states: "What the Servant lifted up on Himself and carried were [our sickness and our sorrows]. Those are not, first of all, our sins (the next verse speaks of them), but rather the consequences of our sin, the sorrows and pain, all the woe and suffering of time and eternity that sin has brought upon us, death, the wages of sin, Romans 6:23."[14] We recall what Matthew said in regard to Jesus healing the many afflicted people who were brought to him: "This was to fulfill what was spoken through the prophet Isaiah: 'He took up our infirmities and carried our diseases'" (Matthew 8:17).

What did Jesus die for? Everything! Sin and the effects of sin. When he died on the cross, he took away the guilt of our sin and everything that God sent on this world as a judgment against sin, and this includes sickness and other physical ailments.

In light of this, are the Pentecostals and charismatics accurate in their claim that just as Jesus forgives all our sins, so he takes away all our diseases? Yes, he does. We can state without a doubt that all sin and evil are taken away in Christ.

Yet at the same time, we must say no, they are not right. Their claim is true, but their timing is way off. The Lord gave the gift of healings to the early church to testify that the kingdom of God's grace and forgiveness had arrived. The healings that he performed served as irrefutable signs substantiating his testimony that he is the Son of God who became also the Son of Man to redeem fallen mankind from sin and to reconcile the world to God. The healings showed that Jesus had power over all creation and had the right to rule over all for the good of the church. People were healed, the dead were raised, demons were driven out, storms were quieted—all because of Jesus' victory over sin on the cross. His physical healings point to him as the eternal spiritual healer that he is.

Yet Scripture never leads us to believe that the effects of sin are going to be removed in this life in the same way as the guilt of sin is removed. The blanket promise of forgiveness will be copied in a blanket release from the curse of sin only when God creates a new heaven and new earth. Then, and only then: "He will wipe every tear from their eyes. There will be no more death or mourning or crying or pain, for the old order of things has passed away" (Revelation 21:4).

On this side of the new heaven and earth, we live in the old order of things. Our citizenship in heaven is secure by virtue of Jesus' forgiveness. But in the old order, sickness, infirmity, and death are still part of life. Recall our discussion in Chapter 11 of Paul's thorn in the flesh, Epaphroditus' sicknesses, and Timothy's many illnesses.

Because the Pentecostal/charismatic spirit has convinced people that miracles and healings are still given to the church today, they must find a reason why some are not healed. Because they promise more than Scripture promises, they must resort to non-Scriptural explanations—hence the talk about lack of faith.

Here is where the doctrine of justification by faith is endangered. If both forgiveness of sins and physical healing (and we could add tongues-speaking into the equation) are made into promises contingent on faith, they both rise and fall together. Some, because they are cured, may conclude that they also have forgiveness of sins, even though they remain unrepentant and engulfed in an ungodly way of life. Others, who have come to faith in Christ but have not been healed, may come to doubt whether they are truly Christians. Those who doubt that they have enough faith to be healed may also come to doubt whether they have enough faith to be forgiven. Will God's gift of forgiveness fail them just as his promise of healing has? And what of the weak in faith? Could their tenuous grasp of the gospel be ruined when they are not healed of their physical ailments?

We admit that many Pentecostals and charismatics struggle with this issue, and some have modified their teaching of the availability of healing for all. But their basic teachings and the promises of many prominent faith healers make it very difficult for the average member of one of their churches to arrive at a scriptural answer to this problem.

We might also add that the Pentecostal/charismatic argument says too much, even for them. That is, if Christ has defeated sickness and death, it would seem logical that the promise of healing would also include a promise that we will never see death. Yet death cannot be stopped. If forgiveness of sins and physical healing here in this life were both ensured through Christ's atonement, wouldn't it be logical to conclude that whoever comes to faith and has forgiveness immediately receives complete healing of all illness, recovery from all injuries, and even the removal of all physical blemishes?

It is up to God whether a sick person is to be healed and to what degree healing should take place. God may put the sick Christian back on his feet again, yet God may at the same time decree that it would be good for the Christian's spiritual health to carry a degree of illness or affliction in his body. It may be God's will to let the sick person die. This is his prerogative. We must always pray for healing yet leave the result in the hands of our God, who works out all things for our good.

Any spirit, however, who leads us away from the certainty that Christ has forgiven all our sins is not the true Spirit of God but a false spirit.

Conclusion

Church fellowship without doctrinal unity based upon God's Word is unionism, and the modern charismatic movement is full of it. The greatest offense is the unionism practiced by Protestant evangelical charismatics with Roman Catholicism to form a united thrust for evangelizing the world. Mission work in league with Roman Catholicism can only spread a teaching of work-righteousness—which is not the work of God's Holy Spirit.

The Holy Spirit is, as we have often stressed, the "Spirit of truth" (John 14:17; 15:26; 16:13). Holy Scripture is his book. The doctrines in it are his doctrines. It would be logical to conclude that any believer filled with the Holy Spirit would, first of all, have a love for the Word and a love and reverence for every teaching contained in it. Simply put, this is love for the truth. How can a person who loves God's truth compromise with false doctrine by joining hands with it in the charismatic renewal? How can true love for God's gospel of forgiveness lead others to join hands with those who deny that very gospel? The true Spirit of Christ is not the source of this kind of love.

The movement robs the gospel of its content and, at the same time, adds to its gospel promises that God does not make. These promises, when not met, cast doubt on the heart of the gospel, justification by faith.

How can a religious movement that promotes the Holy Spirit and his work be so indifferent to the heart of the gospel? The answer to this question can only be because the charismatic movement is fueled by a false spirit. While there are many in the movement who have repented of sin and confess Christ as Savior, this other spirit is leading them into forms of spiritual life that go against their faith, no matter how good and spiritual this spirit may make them feel. This is the tragedy of the Pentecostal/charismatic movement.

14

THERE IS ONLY ONE PENTECOST

Did a second Pentecost begin in 1900 in Topeka, Kansas, at Bethel Bible College? That, after all, is the ultimate question for anyone studying the Pentecostal/charismatic movement, particularly for anyone considering whether this movement is for him.

This question is not merely for individuals to consider. Noncharismatic denominations should consider it also. Perhaps we should be more forceful in stating that opinion. Noncharismatic denominations *must* consider the question. If there is anything to the movement, if there is indeed a more powerful baptism in the Spirit, if God has bestowed on the church of our day the ability to speak in tongues or heal or do miracles, then every church should buy into it. How can a church afford to pass up something that has the potential to spread the

Word as quickly as this movement does? And an even more important question is, if God has bestowed the spirit behind this movement, then who are we to stand in his way?

It is not enough to look at the excesses of the movement and judge it on that basis. All denominations have skeletons in their closets. This book has pointed out some of the excesses in the Pentecostal/charismatic movement, but it has attempted to steer clear of condemning the movement on the basis of those excesses. If we are convinced that God has given tongues and healing to some in the church today, then we should ask that he give us those gifts too. We should resolve to avoid excesses and follow the advice Paul gave the Corinthians on how to use true spiritual gifts. But we should not shrink from that request even if some will question what we are doing.

Is this movement from God? Was there a second outpouring of the Holy Spirit in 1900?

This book has arrived at the following conclusions: The Pentecostal and charismatic movements do not fit the pattern of Scripture. While the movements' excesses do indeed go against Scripture, it is the movements themselves, their teachings and practices, that we are most concerned about.

Consider these points:

- Pentecostal/charismatic Spirit baptism with all that accompanies it does not match the scriptural experience in which the Spirit brings a person to faith in Christ. What the Pentecostal/charismatic movement experiences finds no parallel within the early church.

- Modern tongues-speaking cannot be equated with the tongues of Pentecost Day or with the tongues God gave the church in the years following Pentecost Day.

- The phenomenon of modern "healings" does not match the healings of Jesus and the apostles.

- The personal revelations many in the movement claim to have do not fit the pattern of such revelations as they are described in the early church.

- The unionistic activities of charismatics undermine the teaching of justification by faith.

- The Pentecostal/charismatic movement states or implies that all who are truly born of the spirit can expect to receive both forgiveness of sins and the various gifts of the spirit. This undermines justification by faith by leading the many who do not receive these gifts to call their own faith into question.

We can only conclude that the Pentecostal/charismatic movement comes from a different spirit. The Spirit of God, who bestows his gifts on the church and who leads us to certain faith in Christ, is not the author of a movement whose very essence does not parallel Scripture and whose teachings and practices seriously compromise the teaching of justification by faith in Christ alone.

Luther's words of warning

In Luther's day there were those who to some extent paralleled the modern Pentecostals and charismatics. In particular, they de-emphasized God's written Word and relied on internal visions and revelations. In dealing with them, Luther would not budge from his conviction that the Scripture is the Word of God and that the Holy Spirit works only through the Word, not through heavenly visions, inner light, direct revelation, and the like. Luther's analysis of them remains valid today. In the following quote, Luther is talking about personal revelations, but his words can be applied to the subjective Pentecostal/charismatic experience as a whole:

> Now when God sends forth his holy gospel he deals with us in a twofold manner, first outwardly, then inwardly. Outwardly he deals with us through the oral word of the gospel and through the material signs, that is, baptism and the sacrament of the altar. Inwardly he deals with us through the Holy Spirit, faith, and other gifts. But whatever their measure or order the outward factors should and must precede. The inward experience follows and is effected by the outward. God has determined to give the inward to no one except through the outward. For he wants to give no one the Spirit of faith outside of the outward Word and sign instituted by him, as he says in Luke 16[:29], "Let them hear Moses and the prophets." Accordingly Paul can call baptism

a "washing of regeneration" wherein God "richly pours out the Holy Spirit" [Titus 3:5]. And the oral gospel "is the power of God for salvation to every one who has faith" (Romans 1[:16]).

Observe carefully, my brother, this order, for everything depends on it. However cleverly this factious spirit makes believe that he regards highly the Word and the Spirit of God and declaims passionately about love and zeal for the truth and righteousness of God, he nevertheless has as his purpose to reverse this order. His insolence leads him to set up a contrary order and, as we have said, seeks to subordinate God's outward order to an inner spiritual one. Casting this order [that God gives the Spirit through the Word and Sacraments—AJC] to the wind with ridicule and scorn, he wants to get to the Spirit first. . . .

But should you ask how one gains access to this same lofty spirit they do not refer you to the outward gospel but to some imaginary realm, saying: Remain in "self-abstraction" where I now am and you will have the same experience. A heavenly voice will come, and God himself will speak to you. . . . Do you not see here the devil, the enemy of God's order? With all his mouthing of the words, "Spirit, Spirit, Spirit," he tears down the bridge, the path, the way, the ladder, and all the means by which the Spirit might come to you. Instead of the outward order of God in the material sign of baptism and the oral proclamation of the Word of God he wants to teach you, not how the Spirit comes to you but how you come to the Spirit. They would have you learn how to journey on the clouds and ride on the wind. They do not tell you how or when, whither or what, but you are to experience what they do.[1]

To Luther there was simply no arguing the fact that the enthusiasts, those heavenly prophets, were walking the devil's road instead of standing firm on scriptural ground. Either Holy Scripture is the "lamp to my feet and a light for my path" (Psalm 119:105) or each is a light unto himself as he follows his own imagination. The attitude of God's people must always be, "The unfolding of your words gives light; it gives understanding to the simple" (verse 130).

Scripture's warnings against false miracles

We must take seriously Scripture's many warnings against false prophets and lying miracles. After Pentecost Day, God poured out spiritual gifts on the church. These gifts allowed members to bear witness to Christ in a way that was necessary for that period. In this book we are not suggesting that there never will be times or circumstances in which God chooses to give such gifts to the church. Scripture does not shut the door on this.

But Scripture does call on the church of every age—the early church included—to assess whether a particular miracle comes from God. There will always be miracles. Tragically, there are many who are drawn to them uncritically. Jesus warns us about many who will come in his name doing miraculous signs and wonders: "Many will say to me on that day, 'Lord, Lord, did we not prophesy in your name, and in your name drive out demons and perform many miracles?'" (Matthew 7:22). Yet Jesus makes it clear that he did not send them. He warns us that "false Christs and false prophets will appear and perform great signs and miracles to deceive even the elect—if that were possible" (Matthew 24:24). He warns us about the Antichrist, the lawless one, whose coming will be displayed "in all kinds of counterfeit miracles, signs and wonders" (2 Thessalonians 2:9).

These passages have obligated us to write this book. And our conclusion has been that the Pentecostal/charismatic miracles, as well as the other phenomena that accompany their spirit, do not fit the pattern of Scripture nor do they promote the teaching of justification by faith.

False doctrine ultimately hinders the progress of the gospel

We must again emphasize a point we have been making throughout this book. Whenever anyone turns to Christ in repentance and faith, that person has the true Spirit of God dwelling within him. If the Lord chooses to reach his elect within the context of the Pentecostal/charismatic movement, we rejoice. If God chooses to bear his Word on the wings of a movement of a false spirit—perhaps because that false spirit is producing phenomena that make the movement popular and fast growing—we will leave that up to him. But in the end, the teachings and practices of the false spirit will cause much damage to the ultimate course of the gospel of God's kingdom. The fire of the false spirit always burns over the landscape of a mission field, leaving it harder for future generations to do mission work there.

Pastor Don Matzat, a former leader in the charismatic movement, shared these insights when he was still in the movement:

> Why is it that among so many in the renewal there is such a restlessness, such a striving to find something more? Many in the renewal have gone from place to place to find the true manifestation of the New Testament church, while others with itching ears have attempted to discover new truths, new teachings, new emphases. Many in the renewal have been on this merry-go-round for years. Even though they speak in tongues, raise their arms in worship, pray with eloquence and share their faith with all boldness, their lives are still marked with restlessness, striving and general dissatisfaction.

> Once a person gets stuck on this treadmill, all sense of peace and contentment soon dissipates. The individual is back on the merry-go-round and will never find that for which he is seeking until he learns to rest his life in Jesus as the only source of peace and contentment.[2]

Christ and the Word—the only answer to the world's spiritual needs

One author expresses what he thinks has brought about the Pentecostal/charismatic movement. In "Pentecostal Breeding Grounds," a provocative editorial in *Present Truth,* he says that formalism, dead orthodoxy, ritualism, and uninvigorated preaching actually contribute to the rise of Pentecostalism. The author also gets at the heart of how churches can faithfully do the work God has given them and feed the spiritual hunger of their members.

> The charismatic movement has its roots in all the established churches. We may take pride in our orthodoxy and

detest the pretensions of the gift of tongues, but as Protestant bodies in general, we have operated breeding grounds of Pentecostalism.

Many people cannot endure the dead formality of the "good old" church. Some of them have endured religion as a child endures medicine—it is awful to take. Now there appears to be some life and vitality in the charismatic movement.

Pentecostalism may be a plague and a heresy, but is it any worse than a dead orthodoxy, where scarcely the living breath of heaven even stirs? Let it be remembered that Laodicea, the last Apocalyptic church, is condemned, not for heresy, but for having no fire in her soul. She is neither cold nor hot, and the divine Lover is nauseated. He reproves her for lack of zeal (Revelation 3:19).[3]

Pentecostals and charismatics offer their services for such churches, where they exist. But one author responds to that offer like this: "Fanaticism is no remedy for formalism. Jumping into a steaming kettle over a hot stove is not much better than sitting stiff in the freezer. Let God thaw us out to a normal, healthy, Christian activity in a world of darkness and sin."[4]

How does God thaw us out and promote spiritual health? Through his Word. We are reminded of the effect the Word of the risen Christ had on the hearts of the two disciples from Emmaus. They experienced the effect of the Word on their hearts even before they knew that Jesus had risen and that they were at that moment talking to their Lord. Thinking back to their experience a few hours before Jesus revealed himself to them, they asked each other, "Were not our hearts burning within us while he talked with us on the road and opened the Scriptures to us?" (Luke 24:32). Good scriptural teaching and preaching is like that! It makes the heart burn with sorrow over sin but especially with joy in the gospel.

The importance that our Savior gives to the Word is also revealed in the prayer he addressed to the heavenly Father the night he was betrayed: "Sanctify them by the truth; your word is truth" (John 17:17).

What we desperately need and what the Lord has given us as our greatest treasure are not religious phenomena but good, solid, law-and-gospel preaching from the pulpits of our land, preaching that will make the hearts of our members burn within them. The strength of the church at Jerusalem following Pentecost Day lay not in tongues-speaking but in the Word of the gospel and the attentiveness of the church to the doctrine of the apostles:

> They devoted themselves to the apostles' teaching and to the fellowship, to the breaking of bread and to prayer. Everyone was filled with awe, and many wonders and miraculous signs were done by the apostles. Every day they continued to meet together in the temple courts. They broke bread in their homes and ate together with glad and sincere hearts, praising God and enjoying the favor of all the people (Acts 2:42,43,46,47).

Recall that the Ethiopian eunuch had a problem when he first met the evangelist Philip. He had been wearily trying to understand the Old Testament prophet Isaiah. His mind kept drawing blanks. His problem was solved when Philip preached to him about Jesus. The eunuch went home a new man, filled with immense joy. Why? Because by the Holy Spirit's operating in his heart through God's Word, he had found his Savior. Through the Sacrament of Baptism, he received the gift of the Holy Spirit, who by that same sacrament confirmed his faith in Christ and bestowed on him God's forgiveness. The eunuch's sins had been washed away. He had been born again. His heart was filled with joy and was on fire.

What the church so desperately needs today are people who have a simple and childlike trust in the power of God's Word and sacraments. Our greatest joy would always be that our names are written in heaven and our continued source of spiritual nourishment is the Word of God. In the meantime, we remember the apostle John's words: "Jesus did many other miraculous signs in the presence of his disciples, which are not recorded in this book. But these are written that you may believe that Jesus is the Christ, the Son of God, and that by believing you may have life in his name" (John 20:30,31). We focus on the miracles of Jesus and his disciples and learn from them the spiritual lessons that God intended. And we keep our eyes focused on Jesus, believing that he is the Christ, the Son of God, and rejoicing in the life that we have by his name. And we do all we can to make our churches workshops of the Holy Spirit through the study of his Word.

The so-called second Pentecost that was supposed to have started in 1900 in Topeka, Kansas, fails to measure up in doctrine or practice to the first Pentecost, so we dare not become its children. As God's people we can do nothing better than remain children of the first Pentecost and seek our spiritual nourishment in the powerful gospel that God offers us in Word and sacrament.

ENDNOTES

Introduction

[1]Richard N. Ostling, "Counting Every Soul on Earth," in the religion section of *Time,* Vol. 119, No. 18 (May 3, 1982), pp. 66,67.

[2]Constance Jacquet, *Yearbook of American and Canadian Churches* (Nashville: Abingdon Press, 1983), pp. 225,226.

[3]Harold B. Smith, editor, *Pentecostals from the Inside Out* (Wheaton, IL: Victor Books, 1990), p. 122.

[4]Rev. Dr. David B. Barrett, "Annual Statistical Table on Global Missions: 1993," appearing in *International Bulletin of Missionary Research* (1993), excerpted from *Status of Global Mission, 1993.*

[5]Rev. Dr. David B. Barrett, statistic appearing in "The Twentieth-Century Pentecostal/Charismatic Renewal in the Holy Spirit, with Its Goal of World Evangelization," an article in *International Bulletin of Missionary Research* (July 1988), quoting from Dr. Barrett's *Global Expansion of the Renewal across the 20th Century, A.D. 1900–2000.*

[6]James Lee Grady, *What Happened to the Fire? Rekindling the Blaze of Charismatic Renewal* (Grand Rapids: Chosen Books, 1994), p. 42.

Chapter 1

[1] William Smith and Samuel Cheetham, editors, *A Dictionary of Christian Antiquities: Being a Continuation of the Dictionary of the Bible*, Vol. 2 (Hartford: The J. B. Burr Publishing Company, 1880), p. 2041.

[2] Smith and Cheetham, *Dictionary*, p. 2042.

[3] Benjamin Breckinridge Warfield, *Counterfeit Miracles* (New York: Charles Scribner's Sons, 1918), p. 11. See also Smith and Cheetham, *Dictionary*, p. 2042.

[4] Henry Hampton Halley, *Halley's Bible Handbook: An Abbreviated Bible Commentary* (Grand Rapids: Zondervan Publishing House, 1962), pp. 870,871.

[5] Halley, *Halley's Bible Handbook*, p. 857.

[6] Warfield, *Counterfeit*, p. 11.

[7] Warfield, *Counterfeit*, p. 12.

[8] Warfield, *Counterfeit*, p. 10.

[9] Philip Schaff and Henry Wace, editors, *A Select Library of Nicene and Post-Nicene Fathers of the Christian Church,* Second Series, Vol. 1, translated into English with prolegomena and explanatory notes (New York: The Christian Literature Company, 1890), p. 231.

[10] Schaff and Wace, *Select Library*, p. 231.

[11] Smith and Cheetham, *Dictionary,* p. 2042.

[12] Warfield, *Counterfeit,* p. 12.

[13] Warfield, *Counterfeit,* p. 46.

[14] Warfield, *Counterfeit,* p. 45.

[15] Warfield, *Counterfeit,* p. 10.

[16] Warfield, *Counterfeit,* p. 12.

[17] Warfield, *Counterfeit,* p. 12.

[18] Warfield, *Counterfeit,* p. 10.

[19] Warfield, *Counterfeit,* pp. 61,83.

[20] Warfield, *Counterfeit,* p. 83.

[21] Morton T. Kelsey, *Tongue Speaking: An Experiment in Spiritual Experience* (Garden City, NY: Doubleday & Company, Inc., 1964), p. 183.

[22] Erwin L. Lueker, editor, *Lutheran Cyclopedia* (St. Louis: Concordia Publishing House, 1954), p. 349.

[23] Lars Pederson Qualben, *A History of the Christian Church* (New York: Thomas Nelson and Sons, 1933), p. 317.

[24]Charles Michael Jacobs, *The Story of the Church* (Philadelphia: The Muhlenburg Press, 1947), pp. 263-265.

[25]Qualben, *History,* p. 318. Lueker, *Lutheran Cyclopedia*, p. 668.

[26]Martin Luther, *Luther's Works,* edited by Jaroslav Pelikan and Helmut T. Lehmann, American Edition, Vol. 40 (St. Louis: Concordia Publishing House; Philadelphia: Fortress Press, 1955–1986), p. 110.

[27]Kelsey, *Tongue Speaking,* pp. 52,53. Frank Stagg, E. Glenn Hinson, and Wayne E. Oates, *Glossolalia: Tongue-Speaking in Biblical, Historical, and Psychological Perspective* (Nashville: Abingdon Press, 1967), pp. 59-61.

[28]Kelsey, *Tongue Speaking,* p. 55.

[29]Lueker, *Lutheran Cyclopedia,* p. 394.

[30]Robert Glenn Gromacki, *Modern Tongues*, p. 22.

[31]Philip Schaff, *History of the Christian Church,* Vol. 1 (Grand Rapids: William. B. Eerdmans Publishing Company, 1952), p. 237. Conrad John Immanuel Bergendoff, *The Church of the Lutheran Reformation—A Historical Survey of Lutheranism* (St. Louis: Concordia Publishing House, 1967), p. 216.

[32]Lueker, *Lutheran Cyclopedia,* p. 376.

[33]See Chapter 2, page 38.

[34]John L. Sherrill, *They Speak with Other Tongues* (New York: McGraw-Hill Book Company, 1964), p. 83.

[35]Sherrill, *They Speak,* p. 84.

[36]Sherrill, *They Speak,* p. 84.

Chapter 2

[1]Frederick Emanuel Mayer, *The Religious Bodies of America,* Fourth Edition, revised by Arthur Carl Piepkorn (St. Louis: Concordia Publishing House, 1961), p. 308.

[2]Mayer, *Religious Bodies,* p. 308.

[3]Frederick Dale Bruner, *A Theology of the Holy Spirit: The Pentecostal Experience and the New Testament Witness* (Grand Rapids: William B. Eerdmans Publishing Company, 1970), pp. 40,41.

[4]Bruner, *Theology,* pp. 46,47.

[5]Bruner, *Theology,* p. 42.

[6]Kelsey, *Tongue Speaking,* p. 65.

[7]James Thomas Nichol, *Pentecostalism* (New York: Harper & Row, Publishers, 1966), pp. 46,47.

[8]Gromacki, *Modern Tongues*, p. 25.

[9]Mayer, *Religious Bodies*, p. 309. Anthony A. Hoekema, *What about Tongue-Speaking?* (Grand Rapids: William B. Eerdmans Publishing Company, 1966), p. 27.

[10]Mayer, *Religious Bodies*, p. 309.

[11]Sherrill, *They Speak*, p. 36. Kelsey, *Tongue Speaking*, p. 82.

[12]Kelsey, *Tongue Speaking*, pp. 81,82.

[13]Sherrill, *They Speak*, p. 37.

[14]Nichol, *Pentecostalism*, p. 28.

[15]Sherrill, *They Speak*, p. 37. Nichol, *Pentecostalism*, p. 29.

[16]Sherrill, *They Speak*, p. 39. Kelsey, *Tongue Speaking*, pp. 62,63.

[17]Gromacki, *Modern Tongues*, p. 26. Hoekema, *What about*, pp. 25,26.

[18]Vinson Synan, *The Holiness-Pentecostal Movement in the United States* (Grand Rapids: William B. Eerdmans Publishing Company, 1987), p. 110.

[19]Synan, *Holiness-Pentecostal*, p. 110.

[20]Synan, *Holiness-Pentecostal*, p. 112.

[21]Synan, *Holiness-Pentecostal*, pp. 110,111.

[22]Synan, *Holiness-Pentecostal*, p. 112.

[23]Nichol, *Pentecostalism*, p. 34.

[24]Sherrill, *They Speak*, p. 46.

[25]Bruner, *Theology*, p. 49.

[26]Nichol, *Pentecostalism*, p. 36.

[27]Bruner, *Theology*, p. 49, footnote 38.

[28]Nichol, *Pentecostalism*, p. 50.

[29]Nichol, *Pentecostalism*, p. 51.

[30]Mayer, *Religious Bodies*, p. 310.

[31]Mayer, *Religious Bodies*, p. 309.

[32]Kelsey, *Tongue Speaking*, p. 75.

[33]Kelsey, *Tongue Speaking*, p. 75.

[34]Edith Waldvogel Blumhofer, *The Assemblies of God: A Popular History* (Springfield, MO: Gospel Publishing House, 1985), p. 102.

[35]See Chapter 2, page 30.

[36]Blumhofer, *Assemblies*, pp. 105,112.

[37]Kelsey, *Tongue Speaking*, p. 67.

Chapter 3

[1]Larry Christenson, editor, *Welcome, Holy Spirit: A Study of Charismatic Renewal in the Church* (Minneapolis: Augsburg Publishing House, 1987), p. 17.

[2]Sherrill, *They Speak,* p. 111.

[3]Larry Christenson, *Speaking in Tongues* (Minneapolis: Dimension Books, 1968), p. 16.

[4]Kelsey, *Tongue Speaking,* p. 97.

[5]McCandlish Phillips, "And There Appeared to Them Tongues of Fire," *The Saturday Evening Post,* Vol. 237, No. 19 (May 16, 1964), p. 32.

[6]Gromacki, *Modern Tongues,* pp. 31,145-147.

[7]Bruner, *Theology,* p. 53.

[8]Edward D. O'Connor, *Pentecost in the Catholic Church,* Revised Edition (Pecos, TX: Dove Publications, 1970), pp. 20,21.

[9]Dennis J. Bennett, *Nine o'Clock in the Morning* (Plainfield, NJ: Logos International, 1970), pp. 1-3.

[10]Bennett, *Nine o'Clock,* pp. 4,5.

[11]Bennett, *Nine o'Clock,* p. 2.

[12]Bennett, *Nine o'Clock,* p. 20.

[13]Bennett, *Nine o'Clock,* pp. 20,21.

[14]Bennett, *Nine o'Clock,* pp. 22,23.

[15]Bennett, *Nine o'Clock,* pp. 29,30.

[16]Bennett, *Nine o'Clock,* pp. 33,34.

[17]Bennett, *Nine o'Clock,* p. 40.

[18]Bennett, *Nine o'Clock,* pp. 52,53.

[19]Bennett, *Nine o'Clock,* pp. 46,47.

[20]Bennett, *Nine o'Clock,* p. 50.

[21]Bennett, *Nine o'Clock,* p. 88.

[22]Bennett, *Nine o'Clock,* p. 58.

[23]Bennett, *Nine o'Clock,* p. 61.

[24]Bennett, *Nine o'Clock,* pp. 70ff.

[25]July 4, 1960, p. 77.

[26]August 15, 1960, pp. 53-55.

[27]Sherrill, *They Speak,* p. 112.

[28]Sherrill, *They Speak,* p. 66.

[29]Kelsey, *Tongue Speaking,* p. 9.

[30]Bennett, *Nine o'Clock,* pp. 85,86.

[31]Bennett, *Nine o'Clock,* p. 84.

[32]Bennett, *Nine o'Clock,* p. 90.

[33]Bennett, *Nine o'Clock,* p. 178.

[34]Herbert Mjorud, *Dare to Believe* (Carol Stream, IL: Creation House, 1975), pp. 93-99.

[35]Gromacki, *Modern Tongues,* p. 35.

[36]Joel C. Gerlach, "The Holy Spirit and the Charismatic Renewal," unpublished conference essay (Mequon, WI: Wisconsin Lutheran Seminary, 1972), p. 8.

[37]Larry Christenson, "Lutherans—The 'Man in the Middle,'" *Lutheran Charismatic Renewal Newsletter,* Vol. 3, No. 7 (July 1977).

[38]Larry Christenson, *The Charismatic Renewal among Lutherans* (Minneapolis: Lutheran Charismatic Renewal Services, distributed by Bethany Fellowship, Incorporated, 1976), p. 13.

[39]American Lutheran Church Special Committee.

[40]Commission on Theology and Church Relations of the Lutheran Church—Missouri Synod, "The Charismatic Movement and Lutheran Theology" (January 1972), pp. 24,25.

[41]"Summary Report: Discussions between Synodical Representatives and LCMS Charismatic Pastors," a report by the LCMS synodical representatives summarizing three meetings held at Divine Word International, Techny, IL (December 1984, November 1985, and September 1986), published in *The Christian News Encyclopedia,* Vol. 3 (New Haven, MO), p. 1937.

[42]"A Brief History of RIM," *RIM Report,* No. 15 (May 3, 1992), p. 5.

[43]Larry Christenson and Jay Huckabone, "Between Friends," *International Lutheran Renewal,* No. 134 (March 1991), pp. 1,2.

[44]United Presbyterian Church, Office of the General Assembly, "Report of the Special Committee on the Work of the Holy Spirit [to the 182nd assembly]" (Philadelphia), pp. 22-28.

[45]United Presbyterian Church, "Report of the Special Committee," p. 46.

[46]David J. Engelsma, *Try the Spirits: A Reformed Look at Pentecostalism,* Fourth Printing (South Holland, IL: The Evangelism Committee, Protestant Reformed Church, 1990), p. 2.

[47]Engelsma, *Try the Spirits,* p. 19.

[48]Kelsey, *Tongue Speaking,* p. 105.

[49]Stagg, Hinson, and Oates, *Glossolalia,* p. 13.

[50]Kevin and Dorothy Ranaghan, *Catholic Pentecostals* (Paramus, NJ: Paulist Press, 1969), pp. 6-8.

[51]New York: Bernard Geis Associates, 1963.

[52]Ranaghan, *Catholic Pentecostals,* pp. 9,10.

[53]Ranaghan, *Catholic Pentecostals,* pp. 10-14.

[54]Ranaghan, *Catholic Pentecostals,* p. 15.

[55]Ranaghan, *Catholic Pentecostals,* p. 15.

[56]Ranaghan, *Catholic Pentecostals,* p. 16.

[57]Ranaghan, *Catholic Pentecostals,* pp. 18,19.

[58]Ranaghan, *Catholic Pentecostals,* pp. 20-22.

[59]Kilian McDonnell, *Catholic Pentecostalism: Problems in Evaluation* (Pecos, TX: Dove Publications, 1970), pp. 22,23.

[60]O'Connor, *Pentecost,* p. 29.

[61]Robert D. Brinsmead, "The Current Religious Scene and the Gospel," *New Covenant,* Vol. 2, No. 12 (June 1973), p. 5.

[62]Ralph Martin, "An Interview with Cardinal Suenens," *New Covenant,* Vol. 2, No. 12 (June 1973), pp. 3,4.

[63]O'Connor, *Pentecost,* p. 20.

[64]O'Connor, *Pentecost,* pp. 21-25.

[65]McDonnell, *Catholic Pentecostalism,* pp. 43-46.

[66]Malcolm Cornwell, quoting Kilian McDonnell, editor, *Worship,* Vol. 47, No. 10 (December 1973), p. 616, in *The Gift of Tongues Today* (Pecos, TX: Dove Publications, 1975), p. 75.

[67]Herman Otten, editor, "Catholics Uniting under the Pope," *The Christian News Encyclopedia,* Vol. 3 (New Haven, MO), p. 2993.

[68]Otten, "Catholics Uniting," p. 2993.

[69]Otten, "Catholics Uniting," p. 2993.

[70]Don Matzat, "Entering into Rest!" *Bread of Life,* Vol. 1, No. 6 (March 1977), p. 12.

[71]Matzat, "Entering," p. 12.

[72]*Voice,* Vol. 13 (April 1965), p. 7.

[73]Phil. Gehlhar, "RIM Is More Than Charismatic," *RIM Report,* No. 16 (November 1992).

[74]Gehlhar, "RIM Is More."

Chapter 4

[1]Bruner, *Theology,* pp. 21,22.

[2]Bruner, *Theology,* p. 59.

[3]Bruner, *Theology,* pp. 70-72.

[4]Gerlach, "The Holy Spirit," p. 12.

[5]Bruner, *Theology,* p. 60.

[6]Bruner, *Theology,* pp. 70-75.

[7]Anthony A. Hoekema, *Holy Spirit Baptism* (Grand Rapids: William B. Eerdmans Publishing Company, 1972) p. 10, emphasis added.

[8]Hoekema, *Holy Spirit Baptism,* pp. 10,11, emphasis added.

[9]Hoekema, *Holy Spirit Baptism,* p. 15, emphasis added.

[10]Hoekema, *Holy Spirit Baptism,* p. 20, emphasis added.

[11]Christenson, *Charismatic Renewal,* p. 35, emphasis added.

[12]Christenson, *Speaking,* pp. 37,38, emphasis added.

[13]Christenson, *Charismatic Renewal,* p. 49, emphasis added.

[14]Christenson, *Charismatic Renewal,* pp. 49,50, emphasis added.

[15]Christenson, *Charismatic Renewal,* pp. 50,51.

[16]Bennett, *Nine o'Clock,* p. 115, see asterisk.

[17]Bennett, *Nine o'Clock,* p. 138.

[18]Gromacki, *Modern Tongues,* p. 38.

[19]J. Rodman Williams, "A Profile of the Charismatic Movement," *Christianity Today,* Vol. 14, No. 11 (February 28, 1975), pp. 9-11 [521-523], emphasis added.

[20]McDonnell, *Catholic Pentecostalism,* p. 20.

[21]O'Connor, *Pentecost,* pp. 14,15.

[22]O'Connor, *Pentecost,* pp. 13,14.

[23]Stephen B. Clark, *Baptized in the Spirit* (Pecos, TX: Dove Publications, 1970), pp. 72,73.

[24]Clark, *Baptized,* p. 36.

[25]Robert D. Brinsmead, "The Current Religious Scene and the Gospel," Part 1, "The Burning Passion of the Current Religious Scene," *Present Truth,* Vol. 3, No. 1 (February 1974), p. 11.

Chapter 5

[1]Bruner, *Theology,* p. 84.

[2]Donald W. Basham, *A Handbook on Tongues, Interpretation, and Prophecy* (Monroeville, PA: Whitaker Books, 1971), pp. 15,34,38.

[3]Basham, *Handbook,* p. 23.

[4]Basham, *Handbook,* p. 25.

[5]Malcolm Cornwell, *The Gift of Tongues Today* (Pecos, TX: Dove Publications, 1975), p. 54.

[6]Smith, *Pentecostals,* p. 133.

[7]Cornwell, *The Gift,* p. 53.

[8]Kelsey, *Tongue Speaking,* pp. 219-222.

[9]Larry Christenson, quoting Gerlach and Hine, *Charismatic Renewal,* p. 78.

[10]Bruner, *Theology,* p. 86, footnote 46.

[11]Sherrill, *They Speak,* pp. 107-111.

[12]Smith, *Pentecostals,* p. 84.

[13]Sherrill, *They Speak,* pp. 98-100.

[14]Bennett, *Nine o'Clock,* pp. 166,167.

[15]Bennett, *Nine o'Clock,* pp. 177,178.

[16]Sherrill, *They Speak,* pp. 13,14.

[17]Basham, *Handbook,* pp. 61,62.

[18]Stagg, Hinson, and Oates, *Glossolalia,* p. 15.

[19]McDonnell, *Catholic Pentecostalism,* p. 18.

[20]Bruner, *Theology,* pp. 85,86.

[21]Frank Farrell, "Outburst of Tongues: The New Penetration," *Christianity Today,* Vol. 7, No. 24 (September 13, 1963), p. 6 [1166].

[22]William E. Welmers, letter to the editor, in "Eutychus and His Kin," *Christianity Today,* Vol. 8, No. 3 (November 8, 1963), pp. 19,20 [127,128].

[23]Gromacki, *Modern Tongues,* p. 67.

[24]Michael P. Hamilton, editor, *The Charismatic Movement* (Grand Rapids: William B. Eerdmans Publishing Company, 1975) p. 132.

[25]Sherrill, *They Speak,* pp. 112,113.

[26]Christenson, *Welcome,* pp. 265,266.

[27]Cornwell, *The Gift,* p. 45.

[28]Cornwell, *The Gift,* pp. 47-49.

[29]"Speaking in Tongues," in the religion section of *Time,* Vol. 76, No. 7 (August 15, 1960), p. 55.

[30]"Rector and a Rumpus," in the religion section of *Newsweek,* Vol. 56, No. 1 (July 4, 1960), p. 77.

[31]Kelsey, *Tongue Speaking,* p. 1.

[32]Kelsey, *Tongue Speaking,* p. 212.

[33]Kelsey, *Tongue Speaking,* p. 212.

[34]Cornwell, *The Gift,* pp. 43,44.

[35]Christenson, *Charismatic Renewal,* p. 80.

[36]Hoekema, *What about,* p. 128.

[37]Hoekema, *What about,* p. 129.

[38]Hoekema, *What about,* p. 129.

[39]Hoekema, *What about,* p. 129.

[40]United Presbyterian Church, "Report of the Special Committee."

[41]Bruner, *Theology,* pp. 92-99.

[42]Raymond J. Storms, "I Chose Not to Be a Charismatic," 12th printing (Glens Falls, NY: Raymond J. Storms and Coneco Laser Graphics, 1986), p. 18.

[43]Storms, "I Chose," p. 18.

[44]Gromacki, *Modern Tongues*, p. 41, emphasis added.

[45]Sherrill, *They Speak,* p. 139.

[46]Sherrill, *They Speak,* p. 139.

[47]Sherrill, *They Speak,* p. 141.

[48]Charles M. Irish, quoting from *Acts 29* (Evergreen, CO: Episcopal Renewal Ministries), "Must I Speak in Tongues?" *International Lutheran Renewal,* No. 136 (May 1991), pp. 3,4.

[49]Kelsey, *Tongue Speaking,* p. 3.

[50]J. Rodman Williams, *The Era of the Spirit* (Plainfield, NJ: Logos International, 1971), p. 16.

[51]Sherrill, *They Speak,* p. 146.

[52]Christenson, *Charismatic Renewal,* p. 85.

[53]Richard W. DeHaan, *Speaking in Tongues* (Grand Rapids: Radio Bible Class, 1967), p. 31.

[54]Storms, "I Chose," p. 40.

[55]Christenson, *Charismatic Renewal,* pp. 47,48, emphasis added.

[56]Christenson, *Charismatic Renewal,* pp. 111-113, emphasis added.

[57]Smith, *Pentecostals,* p. 59.

[58]Christenson, *Welcome,* p. 266.

[59]Rev. Delbert Rossin, et al., *RIM Report,* No. 15 (August 1992), p. 1.

[60]Dennis J. Bennett, "The Gifts of the Holy Spirit," in Michael Pollock Hamilton, editor, *The Charismatic Movement* (Grand Rapids: William B. Eerdmans Publishing Company, 1975), p. 18.

[61]Bennett, "The Gifts," p. 23, emphasis added.

[62]Bennett, *Nine o'Clock,* p. 53.

[63]Bennett, *Nine o'Clock,* p. 54.

[64]Dennis and Rita Bennett, *The Holy Spirit and You: A Study-Guide to the Spirit-Filled Life* (Plainfield, NJ: Logos International, 1971), pp. 59,60.

[65]Bennett, *The Holy Spirit,* pp. 61,62.

[66]Howard M. Ervin, *These Are Not Drunken As Ye Suppose* (Plainfield, NJ: Logos International, 1968), p. 105.

[67]Ervin, *These Are Not Drunken,* p. 173.

[68]Sherrill, *They Speak,* p. 80.

[69]Kelsey, *Tongue Speaking,* p. 127.

[70]Christenson, *Charismatic Renewal,* p. 52.

[71]Christenson, *Charismatic Renewal,* p. 38, emphasis added.

[72]Christenson, *Speaking in Tongues,* pp. 55,56, emphasis added.

[73]Christenson, *Charismatic Renewal,* p. 78,79, emphasis added.

[74]"On the Effects of Speaking in Tongues," *International Lutheran Renewal,* No. 39 (February 1983), p. 1.

[75]McDonnell, *Catholic Pentecostalism,* p. 29.

[76]Clark, *Baptized in the Spirit,* pp. 26,27.

[77]Ranaghan, *Catholic Pentecostals,* pp. 221,222, emphasis added.

[78]Ranaghan, *Catholic Pentecostals,* p. 221.

[79]Ranaghan, *Catholic Pentecostals,* pp. 176,177.

[80]Cornwell, *The Gift,* p. 66.

[81]Basham, *Handbook,* pp. 71,72,74.

[82]Schaff and Wace, *A Select Library,* p. 614.

[83]DeHaan, *Speaking,* p. 31.

Chapter 6

[1]Basham, *Handbook,* pp. 15,34,38.

[2]Christenson, *Charismatic Renewal,* pp. 98,99, emphasis added.

[3]Christenson, *Charismatic Renewal,* p. 99.

[4]Christenson, *Charismatic Renewal,* p. 48.

[5]McDonnell, *Catholic Pentecostalism,* p. 44.

[6]C. Peter Wagner, *How to Have a Healing Ministry without Making Your Congregation Sick* (Ventura, CA: Regal Books), p. 215.

[7]Christenson, *Welcome,* pp. 280,281, emphasis added.

[8]Christenson, *Welcome,* pp. 280,281.

[9]Edward N. Gross, *Miracles, Demons, and Spiritual Warfare: An Urgent Call for Discernment* (Grand Rapids: Baker Book House, 1990), p. 153.

[10]Christenson, *Welcome,* pp. 283,284.

[11]William A. Nolen, *A Doctor in Search of a Miracle* (New York: Random House, 1974), p. 250.

[12]Nolen, *Doctor,* p. 254.

[13]Nolen, *Doctor,* pp. 59,60.

[14]Nolen, *Doctor,* pp. 74,77.

[15]Nolen, *Doctor,* p. 81.

[16]Nolen, *Doctor,* pp. 73,83,84.

[17]Don Matzat, "Defining the Substance," *Christian News* (July 20, 1987).

[18]Don Matzat, "Charismatic Healing: Sham or Realty?" *Christian News* (August 3, 1987).

[19]Grady, *What Happened,* pp. 65,68.

[20]Christenson, *Charismatic Renewal,* pp. 105,106.

[21]Grady, *What Happened,* p. 117.

[22]Basham, *Handbook,* p. 105.

[23]Basham, *Handbook,* pp. 112-114.

[24]Don Matzat, "The 'Now Word' of the Lord," *The Christian News Encyclopedia,* Vol. 3 (New Haven, MO), p. 1938.

[25]David Edwin Harrell, Jr., *Oral Roberts: An American Life* (Bloomington: University Press, 1985), p. 481.

[26]Harrell, *Oral Roberts,* p. 481.

[27]Harrell, *Oral Roberts,* p. 481.

[28]Harrell, *Oral Roberts,* p. 481.

[29]Dave Hunt, *Beyond Seduction: A Return to Biblical Christianity* (Eugene, OR: Harvest House Publishers, 1987), pp. 242,243, emphasis added.

[30]Christenson, *Welcome,* p. 28.

[31]C. Peter Wagner, *Special Kinds of Church Growth* (Pasadena, CA: Fuller Theological Seminary, 1984), p. 14.

[32]Gross, *Miracles,* p. 8.

[33]John Wimber with Kevin Springer, *Power Evangelism* (San Francisco: Harper & Row, Publishers, 1986) p. 35.

[34]Wimber, *Power,* p. 37.

[35]C. Peter Wagner, *The Third Wave of the Holy Spirit* (Ann Arbor, MI: Vine, 1988), pp. 39,40.

[36]Jim Roberson, *International Lutheran Renewal* (January 1987), quoted in *The Christian News Encyclopedia,* Vol. 3, p. 1935.

[37]Hunt, *Beyond Seduction,* p. 73.

Chapter 7

[1]Grady, *What Happened,* pp. 124,125.

[2]Grady, *What Happened,* p. 117.

[3]Don Matzat, "Handle with Care," *Christian News* (June 8, 1987).

[4]Matzat, "Defining."

[5]Grady, *What Happened,* p. 100.

[6]Grady, *What Happened,* pp. 116,117.

[7]J. I. Packer, "Piety on Fire," *Christianity Today,* Vol. 33, No. 8 (May 12, 1989), pp. 18,19.

[8]*Calvary Contender* (March 15, 1989), *The Christian News Encyclopedia,* Vol. 5 (New Haven, MO), p. 3359.

[9]Smith, *Pentecostals,* p. 137.

[10]David W. Cloud, "Why Is the Charismatic Movement So Popular?" *Focus* (Sussex, England), quoted in *The Christian News Encyclopedia,* Vol. 5, p. 3341.

[11]Grady, *What Happened,* pp. 171,172.

[12]Joseph R. McAuliffe, "Dominion Work REVIVAL," *Calcedon Report* (December 1994), pp. 14,15.

[13]McAuliffe, "Dominion," pp. 15,16.

[14]Jim Jones, "Holy Laughter Marks Revival Experience," Fort Worth *Star-Telegram,* July 2, 1997, pp. 1A,15A.

[15]Julia Duin, *Charisma and Christian Life,* Vol. 20 (Lake Mary, FL: Strang Communications Company, 1994).

[16]Smith, *Pentecostals,* p. 66.

[17]Smith, *Pentecostals,* p. 66.

[18]Don Matzat, "Name It and Claim It!" *The Christian News Encyclopedia,* Vol. 3 (June 29, 1987), p. 1917.

[19]Hunt, *Beyond Seduction,* p. 79.

[20]Dave Hunt and T. A. McMahon, *The Seduction of Christianity: Spiritual Discernment in the Last Days* (Eugene, OR: Harvest House Publishers, 1985), p. 101.

[21]Grady, quoting Jim Bakker, *What Happened,* pp. 130,131.

[22]Smith, *Pentecostals,* p. 65.

[23]Hunt and McMahon, *Seduction,* p. 183.

[24]Packer, "Piety," p. 19.

[25]Don Matzat, "Enthusiasm Versus Scholasticism," *The Christian News Encyclopedia,* Vol. 3, p. 1916.

[26]Matzat, "Enthusiasm," p. 1916.

[27]Smith, *Pentecostals,* pp. 62,63.

[28]Gross, *Miracles,* pp. 117,118.

[29]Grady, *What Happened,* pp. 103,104

Chapter 8

[1]Grady, *What Happened,* pp. 156,157.

[2]Dennis Pederson, "A New Focus for A.D. 2000," *International Lutheran Renewal,* No. 110 (January 1989), pp. 1,2.

[3]Allister E. McGrath, "Do We Still Need the Reformation?" *Christianity Today,* Vol. 38, No. 14 (December 12, 1994), p. 33.

[4]Vinson Synan, *In the Latter Days: The Outpouring of the Holy Spirit in the Twentieth Century* (Ann Arbor: Servant Books, 1984), p. ix.

[5]Christenson, "Lutherans," emphasis added.

[6]Vinson Synan, "Pentecost Prayer Vigil Meets in Jerusalem," *International Lutheran Renewal,* No. 116 (July 1989), p. 1.

[7]Synan, "Pentecost Prayer," p. 1.

[8]Synan, "Pentecost Prayer," p. 1.

[9]Larry Christenson, "'Brighton, '91' Is God's Idea," *International Lutheran Renewal,* No. 136 (May 1991).

[10]Paul Anderson, "Is the Church a Non-Profit Organization?" *International Lutheran Renewal,* No. 41 (April 1983), p. 2.

[11]Christenson, *Welcome,* p. 198.

Chapter 9

[1]Bruner, *Theology,* p. 263, emphasis added.

[2]Paul E. Kretzmann, *Popular Commentary of the Bible: New Testament,* Vol. 2 (St. Louis: Concordia Publishing House), p. 430.

[3]Philip Schaff, editor, *A Select Library . . . ,* First Series, Vol. 7 (Buffalo, NY: The Christian Literature Company, 1886–1889, p. 498.

Chapter 10

[1]Schaff, *Select Library,* pp. 497,498.

[2]Gromacki, *Modern Tongues.*

[3]Paul L. Maier, *First Christians: Pentecost and the Spread of Christianity* (New York: Harper & Row, Publishers, 1976), pp. 107,108.

[4]Maier, *First Christians,* p. 108.

[5]Maier, *First Christians,* p. 108.

[6]Frederick Fyvie Bruce, *Paul: Apostle of the Heart Set Free.*

[7]Kretzmann, *Popular,* p. 157.

Chapter 11

[1]Wimber, *Power,* p. 6.

[2]Gross, *Miracles,* p. 37.

[3]Don W. Hillis, *Tongues, Healing, and YOU,* Part 2 (Grand Rapids: Baker Book House, 1969), pp. 36-39.

[4]R. C. H. Lenski, *The Interpretation of St. Paul's First and Second Epistle to the Corinthians* (Columbus: Lutheran Book Concern, 1935), p. 503.

[5]W. J. Conybeare and J. S. Howson, *The Life and Epistles of St. Paul,* New Edition (Grand Rapids: William B. Eerdmans Publishing Company, 1951) p. 337.

Chapter 12

[1]Grady, *What Happened,* pp. 91,92.

[2]Lenski, *Interpretation,* p. 578.

[3]John Wimber, *Power Evangelism,* pp. 57ff.

Chapter 13

[1]Gromacki, *Modern Tongues,* p. 44.

[2]Bennett, *Nine o'Clock,* pp. 11,12.

[3]Stagg, Hinson, and Oates, *Glossolalia,* p. 98.

[4]Mayer, *Religious Bodies,* pp. 481-487.

[5]Mayer, *Religious Bodies,* pp. 490-492.

[6]Clark, *Baptized,* pp. 10,11.

[7]Oral Roberts, *The Call* (Garden City, NY: Doubleday & Company, Incorporated, 1972), p. 38.

[8]Roberts, *Call* p. 39.

[9]Bruner, *Theology,* p. 49.

[10]Don Matzat, "Dialogue," *Bread of Life,* Vol. 1, No. 5 (February 1977), p. 12.

[11]Roberts, *Call,* p. 52.

[12]Don Matzat, "Yes a Positive Confession, But . . ." *Lutheran Charismatic,* Vol. 4, No. 2 (February 1978), p. 2.

[13]Christenson, *Welcome,* pp. 280,281.

[14]August Pieper, *Isaiah II* (Milwaukee: Northwestern Publishing House, 1979), p. 440.

Chapter 14

[1]*Luther's Works,* Vol. 40, pp. 146,147.

[2]Don Matzat, "Be Content," *Bread of Life,* Vol. 2, No. 5 (February 1978), pp. 17-19.

[3]Robert D. Brinsmead, "Pentecostal Breeding Grounds," *Present Truth,* Vol. 2, No. 1 (February 1973), pp. 2-4.

[4]R. P. Haakonson, *Filled with the Holy Spirit, Speaking in Tongues, Healing, and Modern Phenomenas in Religion* (Moorhead, MN), p. 7.